And Then What..?

Drewe Broughton

With thanks to author Caroline Allen for her guidance
and support in creating this book.

There's No Destination!

That's the message of this book.

How many people are striving and striving to get the perfect relationship, perfect job, perfect house, right amount of money in the bank, never present always chasing this elusive butterfly.

In And Then What..? Drewe Broughton, a human performance coach and former professional footballer, shares the journey through his life from a boy with dreams to a seventeen career as a professional footballer ending at thirty three years of age, bankrupt, alone, unemployable and contemplating life.

Not being able to control this insatiable desire that "nothing was ever enough." How since retiring in 2011 and spending a month in a rehabilitation centre for addictions and emotional breakdown he has guided some of the world's elite footballers, golfers and business leaders and how as a husband and father he lives by the same wisdoms he shares in the pages that follow.

He explains why we must understand the relentless internal dialogue before we can quieten the voices that make us hesitate and second guess ourselves. That, by understanding and then accepting our complete powerlessness over so many situations we find ourselves in that we can start to harness our true instincts and finally achieve consistency and that potential that we know and feel deep down that we are capable of.

ISBN: 978-1-5272-3259-4

First published in 2018 by Drewe Broughton

Thank-you and a deep, deep appreciation and love to *my mother Trudi*. Her spirit and inspiring capacity for endurance has guided me. She reminded me recently of my relentless curiosity and hunger when back in 2003 I asked her during another bout of desperately seeking answers..

"What is it mum are you born with it or is it made? What is it...?

I'm sorry for the pain I made you go through as only a mother could understand but, that pain was necessary for me to walk into my destiny and today be able to help so many others.

My daughter Talia Grace, who the universe sent to me at a time only the infinite purity and divine love of a child, could have defeated such fear and uncertainty in my soul. I must demonstrate to you the morals and virtues of a man.

Talia- heavens dew.

My wife Helen for her love, belief and support. I have sacrificed much of our time together as I have dedicated myself to not only the writing of this book but, my ongoing work to aid others in their journeys back to themselves and their true paths. It was you who after hearing me on the phone to a client and heard me saying 'And Then What'? Said "And Then what..? That's what you call the book"!

My brothers Gregg and Gareth, who have loved and supported me even when the emotional illness causing my behaviour would have made it so easy to turn your backs. Thank you.

My father Graham. Although not present so much in my life, in my heart I understand why. Lastly, *my grandfather Don.* The cornerstone of our family. I will always remember you and your influence in my life.

A special mention to my friend. My mentor. My spiritual guide has Ron Alfred. Without you keeping me afloat during the stormiest of seas, nothing would have been possible. The phone calls the thousands of miles you travelled all over the U.K. and Europe to "prop me up" I will never, in my heart, in my very being, forget.

The last words you said to me lying there at the end in Milton Keynes hospital back in 2014 will never leave me and guide me today.

'You're a natural born leader. Promise me you'll go and lead'
God bless you Ron. I hope you are looking down and in some way I'm fulfilling today as a coach, what you saw in me as a player.

Trust yourself. Trust what you know.

Sometimes, it is hard to stand in your own truth and trust what we know, especially when others would try to convince us otherwise.

In these cases, others may be dealing with issues of guilt and shame. They may have their own agenda. They may be immersed in denial. They would like us to believe that we do not know what we know; they would like us not to trust ourselves; they would prefer to engage us in their nonsense.

We don't have to forfeit our truth or power to others. That is codependency.

Believing lies is dangerous. When we stop trusting our truth, when we repress our instincts, when we tell ourselves there must be something wrong with us for feeling what we feel or believing what we believe, we deal a deadly blow to our self-worth and our health.

When we discount that important part of ourselves that knows what is the truth, we cut ourselves off from our center. We feel crazy. We get into shame, fear and confusion. We can't get our Bearings when we allow someone to pull the rug from under us. This does not mean we are never wrong. But we are not ALWAYS wrong. Be open. Stand in our truth. Trust what you know. And REFUSE to buy into denial, nonsense, bullying or coercion that would like to take you off course.

Ask to be shown the truth. Clearly- not by the person trying to manipulate or convince you, but by yourself, your higher power, and the universe.

Today I will trust my instincts, and my ability to ground myself in reality. I will not allow myself to be swayed by bullying, manipulating, games, dishonesty, or with peculiar agendas.

Melody Beatty- The language of letting go

Contents

Introduction

And Then What...?

The car windows began to steam up. I didn't look at him. I sat, staring out of the window. It was silent apart from the sound of trucks as they sped past us, spraying the puddles of water that were collecting on the road all over the mud and oil covered verges. My voice broke the silence.

'It's bollocks, it's all fucking bollocks. I hate it all. The money, the job, the pressure, the girls. It's all shit. I just want me back. Where have I gone? I just want to be happy. I hate my life. This was never the plan. None of this was ever the plan. Why, why, why?' My voice was quivering.

I choked back the tears. Less than 24 hours before, I'd walked out in front of 12,000 people. All 6'3, 88kg and 6% body fat of me. I was chiseled and fit. The fitness you can only achieve by dedicating your life to it. But what was the point? What's the point of all of that physical fitness if your soul and mind is so destroyed?

It was another Sunday morning post-match analysis. This one was in the car park of a Little Chef. It was 10.30am and dark; the kind of darkness that only winter brings. It was 5 degrees outside and the rain was relentless as it pounded the car windows.

'I think you're at your best when you attack the near post all the time. You work the box but you've stopped. You're just doing your work up to the 18 yard line. That's the issue.'

"More fucking technical and tactical bullshit", I thought. That's all it ever is, this world and its solutions

The red mist came down. A veil of protection against my fragile soul. I wound the window down, the rain pounded my face. It was coming down even heavier now. The force of air from a passing juggernaut shook the car, but I was oblivious to anything. I wrestled with the clasp on my £6,000 Tag Heuer watch which I'd bought 18 months previously. It wasn't a present or a gift. It was the kind of thing you buy to make yourself feel better. A desperate attempt to look powerful and successful, like I was **the man.** It was all so, so sad. I ripped it off my wrist and in the same ten second rage, pressed the electric window button, releasing the driver side window. The rain poured in. I instinctively threw the watch and all its meaningless fake ness as far as I could. It went over the hedge and into the road I heard it smash as it hit the concrete. A lorry drove straight over the remains.

Ron looked at me. He was worried, he often was. His face was a mix of helplessness, pain and sadness. Ron was one of the cursed humans like me. I say cursed because he was sensitive and compassionate with huge emotional intelligence. Ron was my agent, my mentor, and he had the look you'd give to a wounded dog that you just can't help.

I was a prolific striker from ages 7-18. I scored goals at will. And then, it dried up. I went from averaging 20 goals a season for 10 years. Then I became an 8-12 goals a season man for the next 17 years. The career that looked to be heading to the summit became stale. It's such a familiar tale worldwide. The pain? Oh my God, the pain. The pain of knowing, on the deepest level, that I had the ability to be at the top and to score goals at will, but not knowing how to find it consistently. I fell out of the team as I became more and more desperate. I put more pressure on myself. The misery, the depression. Soon I was drinking, sleeping around and overspending. But most of all, overtraining, over-searching, over training.

'It's killing me,' I said, 'I'm sick and tired of this.' The tears were streaming down my face. 'I'm tired of being tired. I'm 28 now. I've been doing this shit for 12 years. I scored 20-odd goals every season until 18 and now **this.** Year after year of searching. I'm done with it. With all this information, I want to blow my brains out. I need to stop these voices. I can't carry on like this. I'm so fucking lonely. I just played, man, I just ran around. I helped my friends, I helped my manager. I didn't think, I didn't process. I loved it from 7 years of age and now this. Season after season of the same thing happening. It's fucking insanity. It wasn't this hard, it really wasn't this hard.

11

'I'm just tired. I don't want to talk anymore. The team's winning, I'm a substitute but I don't care. I'm just going to go into training in the morning and mess around and have a laugh. I like the boys, but for the last six weeks I've isolated myself. My head talks to me saying 'if you act like them, you'll be average like them' ' got to be serious Drewe, you have to train well, you have to prove to the manager why he should pick you' voices, voices, voices. I'm looking down on everyone. Judging, judging, judging. They're not bad people. I just want to have a laugh and play. I'm done with all this goal setting and targets, and statistics and analysis. I'm fucking done.'

I didn't know what I'd done at the time, looking back now it's one of the major things I do with clients. I had surrendered. I was beaten and powerless over my brain and my thoughts. I wanted out. I laid down my tools and opened my hands to the heavens.

'I'm going to just work hard, it's all I've fucking got now.'

Over the next 10 weeks I scored 7 goals. I dragged my team with me and scouts were flocking. I was a really good player when I was me. Brighton and QPR were interested. Unfortunately, though, there was 14 weeks left. Between weeks 10-14 the wheels fell off. The surrender to my ego, my false fear based self that had happened on that cold November morning on the side of the A5 seemed light years away.

The tragedy was that when I was humbled, finished, I was a very, very gifted human. As the effortless successes came as no games turned to one. One to three, three to five... well by five great games in a row, the voices of my ego would be different voices. " you're the man" " these people wrote you off 6 weeks ago , now look at them " " do you have to run for that ball" " when will I be recognised" " when will the management come to me and say Drewe we really need you, we love you" " this is not enough you need to do more" " it's not this easy". A million voices. Every game that went by when I was back to my true self the ego grew back, stronger more assured. I didn't have a clue that that is what was happening but it was a subtle destructive process. Complacency. The spirit can never be complacent but, it's our attachment to our ego that's the killer. I know today my head is a liar I didn't then. The pressure ramped day by day. " I need to know " I said to Ron, my agent and mentor, " I need to know who's watching , what do I need to do to get them to sign me" every game I went into I had more voices, more pressure, "have to play well, you can't mess up, you must score " I was burning out every week that passed. My ego laughed at me. " you can't keep this up mate, no one will see you playing well, all you do is head the ball and beat people up" I did far more but my lack of trust in who I was latched onto that voice. All of a sudden, no goals, poor performances, I was back to the same place. Four scouts spoke with Ron. Their words haunted me for years in their truth.

'He flatters to deceive.' 'He has everything, but it's too much of a risk.'

During that period I became more and more isolated in my thoughts. I was scrambling to the finish line, the end of the season, if I could just keep it going. My discipline, my dedication, my professionalism, it was too much. I had sheets of paper all over the kitchen cupboards.

Monday to Sunday
8am get up.
9am at training ground
9.15-9.30 breakfast.
9.30-10.15 gym.
10.30- 12.30 train.
12.30- ice baths, recover.
1pm lunch.
2pm go home.
4.30 gym or track... train again
6pm home.

Another sheet. Food, how much water, my 5 supplements. All with a tick box next to them. The mindset? I will control whether I play badly or not. You see if I can be perfect in all i do I will eliminate the risk of failure, of not performing to my best. Constantly convincing myself that it's because I'm a winner and I'm elite and that's what elite do. I had shelves of books. SAS veterans, autobiographies of the best, footballers, athletes, business leaders, trainers... SURELY SOMEONE CAN SHOW ME JUST WHAT IT TAKES TO BE THE BEST?!

I was like that good looking guy or girl you meet and they seem too good to be true. Hard working, funny, kind, beautiful. When it's just you and them you have the best time but, every time they go out with their friends, or they drink, they change. They don't text back and they don't answer your calls. You want to believe in these amazing qualities so you hang in there. Your heart continues to get broken, your faith and trust shattered. Why?

As soon as I started doing well, a voice said, 'I tell you what, have you heard about the teams watching you? If you keep this going you're going to get a really good move. Better money, much nearer the top. Do you even have to run for that ball anymore? You're the main man. You're better than all of them. They wouldn't be winning if it wasn't for you.'

Oh that voice. What did I do? I started thinking. I need to keep this going, I need to keep scoring. I'm better than all of them. From instinct to thought. From love to need. From joy to misery. From glory to pain.

For 33 years of my life I doubted my true self, my instincts, my effortless ease, the quiet, deep inner voice that had led me to so much and so effortlessly and completely that I had abandoned it. As a result of my denial I had violated my inner voice with lies. It had the gravest consequences. In the end, I questioned whether I could trust my own instincts and didn't know what I 'felt' anymore.

It's my hope that through some of these words and stories in the pages that follow, that you can take steps towards returning to the feelings in your guts and heart.

Standing up and speaking from our guts and heart, or playing from our instincts and imagination in the same way we did when we were children, is one of the most difficult things to do. It's a tragic irony.

It's tough to be yourself; your true self.

Our self-respect rises as we do. We develop a better reception for our inner voice and for our creative, natural self as we have the courage to face the truth. As we do, we accept we are never absolutely right but we continue with humility.

I sit here, pen in hand, and I'm motivated to write; to share.

I'm 39 years of age and I spent 30 of those years living, sleeping and breathing football. As a player, as a therapist and as a coach. I want to share my journey; my pain, my lessons, my findings and my hope.

I'm a human being like we all are. I'm perfectly imperfect. These pages will tell you about my journey and about my search. Today I sit here and through much suffering I found the truth. The presence, the deep knowing of who we are and what we are here to do.

For too many years I searched and searched for answers. How can I be the best? What's the magic formula? How can I be quicker/stronger/more knowledgeable? If I sleep more, eat better, do yoga, body building, sprint training - if I'm always different, I thought, I will rise above everybody else and I will be the best. What a myth.

Chapter 1 – Surrender was near

Self-interest is but the survival of the animal in us. Humanity only begins for man with self-surrender.

—Henri Amiel

And Then What...?

May 6th 2011, the day the lid on my coffin finally shut close. The coffin of my dreams, my passion, my love from a small boy. It was finally over. I was standing in the corner of the pitch by the touchline where substitutes warm up.

I watched as the huge digital numbers counted down. They read 89.32, 89.33, 89.34, 89.35. 90 minutes was coming, maybe it'd be 95 today with the substitutions and the stoppages. I thought there would probably be around five minutes of added time. For so many years I came from these positions and turned my destiny on its head by scoring an equalising or winning goal. So many times I came on and was absolutely exhausted, could hardly run and wasted a valuable opportunity to "prove" I was back again , that I COULD be trusted .That's the price you pay for 24 hours of thinking. But today the universe was drawing a line under it all. Today wasn't going to be a day for glory or for one last hit of adrenaline. Today was the last day of a 17 year career. And 25 years of dreams and a purpose.

My soul knew, as it always did, as it always does. It wasn't just the countdown to the last game of the season, it was the countdown to the end of my life as I knew it, my dreams, my addiction and my world.

I would like to say sorry to everybody connected with Lincoln City Football Club. It's a great club with strong heritage and stature in English football. I'm sorry to the management team; Chris Sutton, Ian Pearce, Steve Tilson , Paul Brush and all of the staff, the board, the players and the town.

I was the wise head; the steel and consistency in a young side. I'm sorry for not earning the good wages I was paid. I'm sorry 'boss' for once again flattering to deceive. I'm sorry for going missing and turning in performances that didn't justify your confidence in me.

I'm sorry for being so ill at that point in my career that I lived life so full of doubt and fear. I was so needy and weak that I destroyed the spirit within the dressing room.

I collected my boots and wash bag and walked from the dressing room for the last time. There had been 15,000 fans there that day. It was a must-win to stay safe. We lost. I was an unused substitute. The worst kind. The dressing room after any loss is a morbid place. But, after a relegation when jobs are lost it's like a morgue. It's another feeling that makes a career in professional football so unique. Empty water bottles and energy drinks litter the floor. Banana peels, physiotherapy strappings, mud, towels and all kind of other pieces of shrapnel. The wreckage of a performance that has been built towards for 7 days. For such an emotional game and when so much is on the line like this one, I walked up the tunnel at Sincil Bank, Lincoln, and pushed the doors open to the car park. I was broken. I just wanted to go, to leave and to run away without anybody seeing me. Who was I kidding?

You're paid to take the bullets, you're paid to be public cannon fodder. There was a mob assembled in the car park. A mix of beer, pain, anger, bitterness and sadness. I can't blame them. Being a football supporter is a highly emotive thing. It's like a religion and they pay good money to watch. We'd let them down. I'd let them down; a top paid player, senior spokesman, an apology of a human being that I had become.

'You're a wanker Broughton, you're shit. Fuck off and never come back.' Like a bullet from a gun it punched into me.

'Fuck off, Broughton. You're a disgrace. A fucking disgrace.' Boom, two more bullets punctured my now limped body. I slid into the car and reversed quickly. I braked, spun the wheel and *bam,* something heavy bounced off the window. A rock, I'm sure. I sped out of the carpark and did a right, heading back to Milton Keynes.

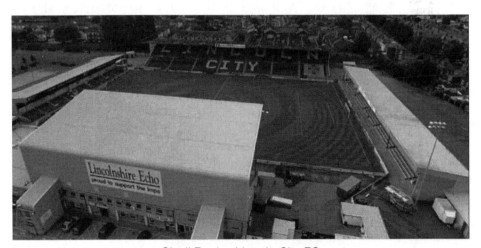

Sincil Bank - Lincoln City FC

Now, you might say that's a normal reaction - get out of there - but no, running, hiding and being so, so scared were symptoms of a slow death. A slow loss of self-worth, self-respect and self-value. You see, during the stages of my career - many of which you will read about in the pages that follow - when I respected who I was, there's no way I would've let that go.

If I'd have looked in the mirror that day knew that I played well and gave everything. Well, then I would've pulled up the handbrake when that rock hit my window. I would've stepped out the car and would've taken on the guy who dared to disrespect me and all the work I'd put in, day after day, to become a footballer. I would've known, walking across that car park that I could take on anybody. One man, two, three; I wouldn't have cared. I was riddled by a thousand fears and self-loathing, though. I exited that car park with my tail between my legs. You see, shame to the spirit is like cancer to our physical bodies. It eats us alive from the inside. It destroys self-value and worth. It casts dark clouds over joy and serenity.

Toxic shame is to feel flawed and defective as a human being. Well, I certainly felt that. At 5.45pm on May 6th 2011 I was riddled with it. In my head, in my heart, I was pond life. The lowest form, a joker and a defective human being. Years of dishonesty to so many and the worst case to my self-caused shame. To quote Al Pacino in his Oscar winning performance in SCENT OF A WOMAN "You see I always knew the right path, without exception I knew. But I never took it. You know why? Because it was too damned hard" so my self-worth was on the floor, intact lower than the floor. Self-worth comes from walking the right path. Never selling out. Never buying in to others opinions of you or advice. As I drove out of the stadium, grief descended over me quickly. I had a real sense of loss. It was real, so real. The feelings were beyond those of which I could deal with. I caught the sight of the golden arches of McDonalds in the corner of my eye and sharply turned it. Excitement, a spike of adrenaline. It was a spark of light into a deadened human being.

My whole spirit lifted as I said, 'Big Mac Meal, please. And a milkshake and large fries.'

'Is that all, sir?'

'Ummm.' I paused.

'Sir?'

'No, a McFlurry and three chocolate doughnuts as well... Actually 6 doughnuts, give me 6 please'

'6 sir? Did you say 6 doughnuts'?

It's like that questioning was a mirror getting held up to the void inside so huge that I was being made to look at it. I had been made many times before, but, like many people, I had turned my back on the sheer vastness of the task to fill it.

In little over 15 months from that day I would embark upon a journey which made me understand the pause before making the decision to take the McFlurry and doughnuts. I'd understand that when one's spirit is bankrupt and the void inside is so huge, nothing can fill it. The pursuit of constantly trying to fill it with food, alcohol, girls, clothes, glory, fame , with stuff, with meaningless goods would ensue.

I pulled out of McDonalds, ramming fries into my mouth. I could feel the sugar in the food releasing endorphins into my spirit and giving me a temporary high. Football gave me that high. When I couldn't find the form to get my high from football, that's when the spending, the shopping, the sex and the eating would begin. It was all to fill that void in my soul.

I was half way through the journey, when, through nothing more than distraction after the sugar hit had worn off, I turned on my phone. Every footballer will relate to that moment, post-match, when you turn on your phone. If you played well, a million well-wishers. The people who haven't spoken to you for weeks and months come out of the woodwork. If you haven't played well, or even worse, haven't played at all, you dread it. The sympathy, the fear, the advice, or, often there are no text messages at all. There's such a fickleness to it all.

I saw 12 pending text messages. I left them unanswered. The phone rang. On the screen 'Mum Home' flashed up.

'Are you ok?' She said. My poor Mum; she has shared this journey with me from the start.

One time, she told me she was always worried about me in that motherly, instinctive kind of way. She knew there was a sensitivity to me, coupled with a bravery and a jump first, ask questions second mentality. What mother wouldn't worry with that cocktail of emotions?

'Yeah, I'm just on the way home Mum.'

'We were listening on the radio.' Mum was looking after my grandparents at this stage. My Grandad would always listen on the radio with my Mum. "Pop" was a family hero, many have one. A Self-made multi-millionaire, they had lived all over the world, a wonderful life. He didn't make his beloved Air Force in World War two due to his hearing impediment. Was army champion 1500m and cross country. Represented the forces nationally in war time for football and had trials with Sheffield United pre war. He knew me on that deep level. I was wired that way. Their hearts and minds were purely on love and support. Yet, this thought, post-match, just adds more pressure. I felt a need to validate, to answer, and to try to explain feelings and experiences that could never really be grasped.

I learnt that bearing my soul just brought fear to those who haven't walked the same path as me or taken on a similar journey.

'Why didn't they just put you on? Stupid man. Well, he got what he deserved.' Mum's fierce love and loyalty to her son coupled with the ruthlessness that I'd shown as well, came out in her comments. I'm sure so many Mothers worldwide would say the same.

Yet, my honesty would always create a discomfort on hearing those things. The great irony is that whilst my capacity to endure painful truths borders on masochistic, I also had great areas of dishonesty in my life as I scurried and ran to cover the holes left by escapism. If I had a pound for every time my Mum said 'why didn't they put you on?'

'Oh well, onwards and upwards.' She said. I love my Mum. Her spirit in her endeavour is heroic. The sacrifices she made for me and my brothers from young children epitomises the spirit of an amazing lady. But, I knew there was no onwards and upwards from this one.

Chapter 2- The death of my former self

When a man's self is hidden from everybody else ...it seems also to become hidden even from himself, and it permits disease and death to gnaw into his substance without his clear knowledge.

—Sidney Jourard

And Then What...?

I drove back to Milton Keynes down the A1 with a car full of boxes. I was riddled with the voices of fear and uncertainty whirling around in my head. Another season out of contract, another summer of waiting and hoping. No offers came.

From May 6th - June 16th I was in agony. I'd put on two stone in weight. Ice cream, beer and cookies became my staple diet. I'd spend hours making excuses and going to sit by myself on benches. My relationship was a mess; how could I possibly build intimacy when I couldn't even look at myself. I was so dead inside and I'd built up such a wall around myself.

On June 10th, the old warrior spirit growled; 'it's time to go again, big man'. I drove to Nottingham five days a week for a month to train with my trainer and friend, Jake Attwood. On the first day, when I measured my body fat, he just gave me that look. He knew me well by that point. I didn't know how I was going to get through that next month, physically or emotionally, but I did. I lost the weight, I got fit and I was ready to go again. It was a brutally painful four weeks. Physically and emotionally. I know today that I am so so tough at a core level and my spirit can endure almost anything if it's focused on an outcome. A great gift now I have is to understand who the "I" in the "I am" statement actually is. Driven by the fear of no money, the fear of quitting, the fear of failure, the fear of being finished; the fear of everything I turned a flabby soul and body back into a machine to deliver a result.

It would be about 14 months from now - September 2012 - when my world would change. When I would learn more about spirituality, myself, my lost self and the human fundamentals of faith. But the universe still had another year or so to teach me

It was June 28th. That time just before players report back for another 10 month season. Or out of contract players sit by their phones waiting for that call from their agent to say there's a deal on the table. Some security. Some sanity. Some hope. My candle was flickering, just about alive after a brutal months graft when the phone rang that day.
My representative called; 'It's not good, Drewe. Your reputation is really bad.'

I knew it deep down.

'I'm not done.' I said. A familiar retort when told by anyone other than my spirit that the end is here. That finally, finally it's over. You see when you discipline and sacrifice the way I had for the last 4 weeks you EARN belief. I had earned it but this time as I said those words "I'm not done" I'm not sure I really believed them anymore. I thought I would just train, keep fit and wait for a change. It always comes; I'd been doing this for over 15 years.

The next 12 months were painful. I was full of fight and spirit that I will divulge over the following pages. My will, not the will of the universe, dragged me from club to club in the semi-professional game. The addict in me screaming; 'If you score goals, people will see you're back and you will get back into the professional game. You can still get to the top.'

I was running on empty; my soul broken.

I wasn't taken on by Luton Town, After what I thought was a really strong three weeks, goals , great performances and integration to the group. Looking back that deal was never going to come. Everyone knew I could "flatter" but I would soon "deceive" just like an unfaithful partner who when , their back is against the wall and they are clinging to the relationship , would present, what , In often times , was the true person that one partner had fallen in love with, I would soon "cheat" again. Like many in relationships and certainly the way I was in them, not because I'm not a great person and trustworthy, more I didn't have a clue who I was never mind being consistent in my behaviour or performance.

I was signed and released by Alfreton Town. Managed by a man I have so much respect for, Nicky Law. I had played with his son Nicky junior, a really talented player. Nicky backed me, they paid me well. I Was expected merely to turn up on a Saturday, as I lived 100 miles away and give the team some of that "cutting edge" that "streetwise ness" and "aggression" that was the simple remit. Two games. Two red cards. They were unjust but, hey, there's zero complaints. If ever the universe was beating me to my knees it was now. The chairman, a good man. A hardworking man. Sent a simple letter stating that "my behaviour would not be accepted at his club" I understood. The way Nicky dealt with it was top class. He knew that you can't have one without the other. Edge without falling off. You hedged your bets that the guy will walk the right side of the line most of the time. You know it comes with times he will fall off. That last red card actually came on a day at Grimsby town where I played really well. Alfreton played well. I got after the centre halves. They knew me. I had a reputation. They didn't

And Then What...?

know how broken and scared I was by that stage in my soul. 91st minute, long ball up, I jumped early, as I always did, my arm clipped the guy in the jaw. Just a clip. He went down in squealing heap. I had been here so many times. It's a strange moment. It's like you are having an out of body experience. Commotion kicks off. Players flood to the referee like vultures to a carcass. You are standing 10 yards away. Watching the carnage, the desperation, the judge and jury. You are always in a quiet awareness when you've been there a few times. On that day it was my 17th year and 14th red card. I knew immediately. Sometimes you look for the bench to catch the mangers eye. I had learnt over the years, 99% of them are so disgusted they look the other way or pretend they can't see you. They chuck you to the wolves. Not that day. I caught Nickys eye. There was that look of pity. He was a tough guy, he knew through experience that on some days they go against you. He also knew that was me done. I did to.

I boarded yet another coach. Pulled up outside the dressing rooms at Grimsby town FC, the doors to the coach were open. I had got onto several coaches pulled up in this very same position since 1996. Good days and bad. A plethora of emotions always accompanied you. Huge highs, an enormous relief many times, other days in this same spot a low the likes of which I felt today. "You again" that voice inside cranked up again. My fight back usually felt stronger. Not that day. I climbed aboard the coach and head down I took my seat next to the window. My forehead pushed against the glass, the coldness of the window was a like an anesthetic to the voices. There was a group of lads standing outside, they looked up , My eyes met those of one the boys. He instantly laughed I could hear it all through the glass ' hahahahahaha you wanker Broughton. You're shit' his mates now joined in. I knew I was finally beaten. Rather than react, I just slowly pulled the curtain. The irony was that the curtain on my brief spell at Alfreton Town was being drawn to. The worst thing about those meaningless boys shouting abuse at just another "footballer" was that they were actually confirming what I thought of myself. I am a useless piece of shit. I am crap. I am a lower league thug. I am a pointless meaningless human being.

I closed my eyes and tried to just sleep. I wanted to just sleep. Maybe to never wake up. What was the point? I had a dream this wasn't it, this wasn't it. My dreams had become a living hell.

26

The club sent me a letter "relieving" me from my duties as a player. I sunk into another deep depression.

I joined Thurrock FC in the Conference south. I respect all people and players but, that was such a low. I never envisaged myself out of the professional leagues. I had had a few loan spells in the 'non-league' as a young player but that was to gain vital playing time and to, I hoped, use those spells as a shop window to sell myself back to bigger clubs. That had worked at the time but, the man that pulled on the number Nine jersey in those days had purpose. I was a shadow of that man. So riddled I was with shame.

So that spell at Thurrock was terrible. Training two evenings a week. I was broken. My whole life to date, there had been a goal, a purpose, a drive. Now what was it? Just pay the bills. It was horrific for a man as ambitious as I was and am.

It was 3 months after joining that the call came. Another club "releasing" me. By now I was so full of shame and grief. I couldn't even get in a team four leagues outside the four professional leagues.

I coached briefly at a school, as I finished my studies on human movement. I had been studying for four years.

During this year I was coaching at a professional academy also. I wasn't sure if this was a new career, as a manager. I loved it. Me, the players, these fourteen year olds as I once was. Who needed to know, were desperate to know, how to "make it" we won nearly every match. Beating Liverpool and Tottenham alongside other big scalps. We were a league two academy. However, I couldn't deal with the politics. I couldn't watch the system stifle and break more guys.

I then had a spell at Arlesey town. This time four leagues down from the last of the four professional leagues. So in affect the eighth division.

The manager there like all the others saw the 'big man' on the outside and not the broken six year old boy inside when after one game I had been totally dominated physically and mentally by a young player on the opposition team, he did what they all did. At half time. Attacked. It was a far more tame verbal attack than the majority I had had over the last seventeen years in bigger stadiums and dressing rooms but, there was no pulling to the side. Asking me privately 'are you ok big guy'? 'You look a shadow of the player I remember'

It was now February 2012. My daughter, Talia was born. I was so scared. So afraid. I had nothing. No career, pay check to pay check. No future. Ok, I was about to qualify as a "movement specialist" but, I had to get that to pay.

In the early days of my daughter being there I was so absent emotionally. It was six months from that month I would first hear the phrase "spiritual bankruptcy" I remember the relief in hearing a diagnosis. One that made total sense.

Out of the blue I got a call from Darlington FC. The manager an ex player there and club legend, another good man, Craig Liddle, called me.

'Hi Drewe. It's Craig Liddle from Darlington FC'

Now I knew Darlington. A club with heritage. With standing but another club on its knees. I had battled them many times over the years in the professional game.

'Big man we are on our knees, in liquidation, the clubs fighting day by day, we have 13 games to

Go. We can't even field 5 subs. The staff had a meeting after Saturday's game and said we are doing well but we are too nice, we just need a big horrible bastard. Someone said we need a Drewe Broughton. So I'm calling you, what are you doing? '

I was sat in a service station on the M6 staring out of the window on a cold grey February Monday. I was on route to see a perspective client. A premier league player who had had recurring groin issues. I was now trying to build a business alongside playing part time.

"Sitting in the car Craig currently"

'you still playing??' he said

'Playing on a Saturday locally for Arelsey Town, just supplementing my income whilst I build my new business'

' Look, here's the script, 13 games left, no players, well about 14 but made of young lads with a few old heads. I can't sign players, there's a transfer embargo. I can only bring in lads who aren't contracted, but I have a pot of money from the administrators. We can stay up but we need fight, some leaders. This club has been a big part of my life, I will do whatever to keep them afloat. If we go down mate it's bleak. Redundancies on mass. Kicked out of the stadium, the end of this great club'

Me in a home game at Darlington. Fighting for more than the club. Fighting to stay alive.

'I'm in' I said

'Fantastic' said Lids

'Get the train up on Wednesday we can put you up and give you £X per match, train Thursday, Friday every week, It's a great club this Drewe and we have some fantastic young lads, but they need some men to help them through'

Not sure I was much of a man any more. Inside I was broken. But, I had been offered a lifeline, a respirator to a dying soul, a defibrillator to an old warhorse, the chance of a battle and glory maybe. I will take 100-1 against, done it all my life, Gambling wasn't my drug of choice or no choice but, I'm a gambler as much as any addicted gambler is, I've always gambled with knowing that if the true me turns up anything is possible the awful shame was that I didn't know how to get him out though.

I actually found the "old me" a few times during that 10 weeks. Luton Town at home. Ironically my local team, the team I grew up watching.

The team I was employed by to coach in the academy. Well that night I practiced what in the week I was preaching. It was a bitterly cold March evening. Luton were desperate for three points. I dominated them and missed a sitter in the 90th minute to have one more feeling of glory.

There was a day away at Telford FC. Managed by former England intentional Andy Sinton, Telford were riding high. A really compact and nice stadium, modern. It had a feel of a professional match. I had eight matches now, so match fitness, that vital component was there. I was brilliant. Aggressive, full of running, free, I scored, made one, had other chances and bullied their back four. Ironically it was a mistake by current England goalkeeper, Jordan Pickford, on loan from Sunderland FC, on that day that cost us. You could see he was top class. I remember his character. What a tough situation for a young man. But he had a real presence.

Ironically that summer Andy Sinton called me and offered me a contract on the back of my performance. Typical Drewe Broughton. When the real me turned up I always gained admiration from guys who had played at the very highest level, I had it in me to be at that level, they knew it.

It would all end for me at Forest Green Rovers. The last time my feet crossed the white lines of a competitive match.

Late April 2012. The club already, relegated, I'm not sure why I played? Pride, desperation, loneliness, I'm not sure.

They were good. A big pitch they were young and athletic.

For twenty minutes I got beaten to every ball by their young centre half. My spirit was dying. This young guy I would have eaten up and spat out a few years, even a few games ago.

A ball was played over the top of their back four. I turned and chased it. The ball was between the defender and the out rushing goalkeeper. I was behind the defender and at that moment a complete emotional build up gripped me. Frustrated at how far I had fallen. Scared of my future. Grieving the end. Knowing the truth. Failing as a father.

My right fist clenched I reached around his body and hit him with a right hook to the temple. He went down.

The pandemonium began. I knew this scene well. My mind flashed to all the trauma of past situations that mirrored this. The moments where I had lost control of the beast within.

I could hear the uproar from the opposition players, from the management. I remember it feeling like an out of body experience.

I looked and saw the look on Craig Liddles face. It was the same look I saw 6 months before on Nicky Laws face. They knew what they were getting.

I walked straight from the pitch, I didn't wait for the referee.

I knew.

I got in the shower. There was twenty minutes to go until half time. I wanted to be out of there before the players got back. Too much shame.

I got to the car park. Started the car and pulled from the car park.

I rang Ron. There was no one else. I had no one else.

We hadn't been working the way we did for so long when there was hope. Ron gave up the ghost eighteen months before when I signed for Lincoln City. He knew.

Ron had been diagnosed with leukaemia.

I was not only grieving the end of my dreams. My best friend, my father figure, my crutch, my light in the dark, could die.

He was in a cancer unit in oxford.

I pulled in and I sat with him.

The tragedy of spiritual bankruptcy is the selfishness. Here was my best friend, dying and all I could do was sit in my misery. I didn't want it to be like this.

The next 4 months months went past. I had built a business offering assessments and solutions to repetitive injuries and physical issues suffered by top footballers. Between business partner, Jake and I, we were seeing ten players. Premier league and internationals at their houses. It started with a few mates. They all respected me. They all liked the man I was at core but, they had kept their distance as the years had gone on. The unpredictability of my nature, the lows and misery weren't nice to be around.

Money was coming in. Slowly. There was a glimmer of hope. However, the real me was still buried. Like a body buried under the wreckage of a fallen building, my spirit, my true self was buried. I was miserable and alone inside. I was growing more and more isolated.

I called Clarke Carlisle (chairman at the PFA, the players union) and we met. He recognised the issue. He called Sporting Chance, a Rehabilitation clinic set up by former England captain Tony Adams to deal with addictions and emotional breakdown. Within days I was on route to Hampshire for an assessment.

My wife at that time couldn't stand my misery; I don't blame her. She was struggling too. I moved out. I had nowhere to go, so I stayed on friends' floors and sofas. During that period I knew I needed some serious help.

I had suggestions from so many people to see a Doctor; get some tablets, get some help. You see, I'd stolen the trust from everybody close to me; not because I'm not a good man, not because I wanted to, but I was powerless - completely and utterly powerless - over the need to escape this internal pain. The agony of what I knew I could be, yet with absolutely no ability to be able to be that man consistently.

Chapter 3 - The Road to Surrender & Enlightenment

The processes of becoming more human, becoming a real person, and finding spiritual enlightenment are very similar. They require slow growth over time.

In September 2012, 15 months on from that relegation with Lincoln City I was finally defeated. The 15 months since May 2011 were a testament only to the strength of the soul within my now broken body and mind. I prolonged the agony, but now it was the end. The pain was so, so vast.

I'll never forget that drive down to the sporting chance clinic in Hampshire. There was hope. I was driving into the unknown, but there was hope. Hope that I could save my marriage, hope that I would see my daughter grow up, hope after 30 years of relentless voices that sabotaged my gifts and voices that destroyed my instinct and intuition, that I could be saved.

My satellite navigation system broke my train of thoughts. I knew I was getting near. Anticipation, nervousness of the unknown, fear, excitement...

'The destination is ahead. In eighty yards turn right.' I applied the brakes gently.

My aggression had gone. I was beaten. A small clearing appeared and I turned sharply into my destination. A long winding road through a dense wood unfolded, the speed bumps gave me a sense of peace. Speed, aggression and self-reliance weren't needed here.

'I'm in the right place.' I thought.

Slow. Peaceful. Natural.

After about a mile I saw a big house, the sat nav was no longer needed.

'Go past the big house. The road bends to the left and you will see a small track, go down here and about 400 meters on the left you'll see a gate and a cottage. Pull into the drive and knock on the door.' I will never forget those instructions.

I had scribbled them down seven days earlier. I hadn't needed to bring the piece of paper. I remember reading them to myself when I came off the phone that day and thought how peaceful it sounded. I had always felt calm in nature. The irony is for so many years I could never enjoy anything; walks in the woods, bike rides, holidays, meals out, PLAYING FOOTBALL. I had ruined every social occasion as I was trapped in my mind. Trapped. Alone and drowning in thoughts.

Psychologists I had paid and used just led me to more thoughts. One of the terrible inflictions caused by depression is the inability to be present. I was *in* the room but was never *in* the room. *On* the pitch but rarely *On* the pitch. *In* the relationship but never *in* the relationship.

I remember being on holiday with a partner and was so absent consumed by thinking , I think I had an emotional breakdown. In the middle of the night staring into the darkness , I started sobbing. Sobbing and sobbing , tears flowed and I , for the time being , had got out a lot of pain. However I didn't realise why I had so much. That was to reveal itself shortly.

I pulled the car slowly through the gates and into the drive. The gravel crunched beneath my tyres. It all became real. Very real. I wasn't a footballer. I was a man, whose life was a mess. In every way a mess. I turned the ignition off. Not even the car was mine. A year ago when the career finished and the contracts dried up, my father in law at the time gave me his. As I took the key from the ignition the shame flooded over me. I don't even own a car. The last traces of what ego I had left slipped away. I was a pathetic excuse for a human being. The cruel byproduct of shame is self-loathing and mocking.

The gravel crunched under my feet as I walked to the small black gate on the side of the cottage. I found myself wanting the gravel to be quiet. It was highlighting my every move.

I knocked on the back door and was greeted by James. James would become my pillar of hope. A role I'm sure he carried and carries with every client he had and has. I was bankrupt financially but the biggest bankruptcy was to be found in my spirit.

'Hello mate.' James said in that gravelly voice.

I awkwardly stretched out my right arm to greet him. Almost instinctively he was inside my arm and put two arms around me.

'Nice to meet you, Drewe.'

He had hugged me. My body was a mixture of tension and relief. The tension a social conditioning on how we greet, and fear. The relief? This guy was going to rescue me.

James West, Clinical Director at the sporting chance clinic and I outside the cottage that was to be my home for thirty days in 2012.

Hugging sporting chances clinical director James West

Two hours passed by in a blur. I had answered a series of questions. It didn't feel clinical. There were soft furnishings; two armchairs in a small quiet room, a large window that looked out into the forest beyond. Light years away from a cold training ground where , you are calmly given a different coloured "bib" by one of the coaches and told to line up against the first team when inside you know on your day you're the best player at the club yet you have no idea how to find that player, that performance.

My friends' words just weeks before echoed around in my head and made me guarded of my answers.

'Don't let them put that God shit on you.'

I waited for 2 hours for the dreaded "G" word. It never came.

'You're not drinking, taking drugs or gambling but wow me, you're as sick as any addict I've ever met.' James said.

That's why I and so many warmed to James. He had his own style, own way, own vocabulary with me, and with other athletes. We were competitive people. A few 'fucks' made us feel like he was on our wave length. Having sat with many therapist and psychologists, all of which were very skilled and competent in their own right, I always felt that my ruthless, competitive 'gift' was always something that they couldn't relate to. James could relate.

'Well, I'm pleased to say we start on Monday. Check in is at 10am. I would love to see you here. Addicted to love, addicted to sex and addicted to football. Don't worry, we will find where you fit in.'

It was the greatest relief; salvation! I didn't know what I was walking into, I had no idea what lay in the month ahead or what my life would look like beyond the 30 days. But, from nights sleeping on the sofas of friends and family, sandwiched between cold nights sleeping on the back seat of my father-in-law's car, there was a warm bed and a light, albeit barely flickering but a light nonetheless.

I felt relief flood my body, finally somebody might have the answers; the answers I've looked for all of my life. I remember driving down there on the Monday morning. I had a simple sports bag with a few clothes and a wash bag. I didn't own much at that stage.

I don't want to name and shame anybody. That's not what this book's intention is. The people that called me had one genuine concern; *'Please, please don't let them turn you to God and religion.'* They said. I'd not even considered this. Shit, I thought. What would happen with God and religion?

The pain I'd suffered most of my adult life was unbearable. The last 15 months were full of nights where I lay staring at the ceiling, pretending the next day that I'd slept. The hours turned to days, time just passed by. But the greatest pain of all - the one that had even suggested death as a viable option - was the pain of unfulfilled potential. Of me turning my back on my destiny.

As I checked in for my 30 days in the middle of that forest in Hampshire, I only felt relief. Yes I was scared, yes I was apprehensive but I was tired and broken. I finally wanted help and, in the safety of that place, I thought I might find some answers here.

At 33, bankrupt, alone and with not one thing I could attach to, I had to gain a sense of who I was.

'Who am I?'

My notes from sporting chance

It was the first time. The first time there was no escape. Me. 30 days. A pen, paper and the truth. Finally the truth. My pen flowed, the truth flowed. There was nowhere else to run. Life had flushed me out to be cleansed and start again.

'All is well.' The quiet whisper said. I listened to that voice, not with my ears, but with my heart and my instincts, my very essence.

Finally, I was ready to become the man I was always meant to be. All the rabbit warrens I had run down for years and years only to hit another false alarm, another dead end. Finally, this path felt right.

I was scared. I was so vulnerable, so naked. I realised that that is how I came into this world and at 33, I had been led back to my very essence, my true self.

The thirty days that unfolded were a mixture of excruciating loneliness, pain, suffering, hope, humility, desperation, sadness, grief and many other emotions as the death of my former self occurred. It made way for the rebirth of my true self, blocked by a thousand forms of fear, resentments, dishonesty and desperate self-seeking behaviours.

The days started to take structure. A structure I had missed like many former athletes, ex-servicemen, mothers and the retired can all relate to.

I would get up 7.30am, we would convene in the small lounge downstairs. There were three sofas. We would take a seat. One of the boys would make tea. We would sit in silence and wait for James. The therapists would stay in the cottage next door or return home daily to come back in the mornings.

I will never forget that first morning.

'Good morning gentleman.' James said softly.

'Drewe, how are you this morning?' There was a pause. The voices in my head begun.

How am I? How fucking am I? I'm homeless, I'm bankrupt, my career is finished and at 33 I'm sat here in fucking rehab! How do you think I am?

Instead I said, 'Erm, I'm tired, erm, I am.. ummmmm ... I am... ok.'

'Thank you Drewe. Ok isn't a feeling. How do you feel?'

'Ummmmm.'

The umm said it all. I didn't know. I didn't have a clue how I felt. I hadn't been allowed to have my feelings for a long, long time.

'I'm scared. I'm afraid. I am so, so afraid.' The words softly left my lips.

I had surrendered. Surrendered to the ego. I didn't know it. But that's what was happening. The ego can't survive where there is truth and presence. It's impossible. The ego sits in morbid reflection of the past or irrational fears of the future.

'Thank you, Drewe.' James said. 'Mark, how do you feel?'

It continued like this day after day for 30 days. After the meeting I would have breakfast. And then I would run. The forest was vast and beautiful. I would use the gym and pool. It was a three pronged attack on a withering human; mind, body, soul. No junk food in the cupboards, no escapism through sugar.

We would be left with no other choice than to get better. We would have daily 1:1 therapy. We would be given a workbook that would become our sanity. The therapy was based around the twelve step model of Alcoholics Anonymous. Step one; admitting I am powerless over a behaviour. Step 2; believe in a power greater than me. Step 3; make a decision to hand over my will and life to this power. Now it took a while for me and others to investigate steps 2 and 3. But we had 30 days. Step 1 was completed on night one.

We would go to 'meetings' in the evenings. Village halls, church halls, central Chelsea meeting venues. The affliction of addiction, of spiritual bankruptcy affects many. It's a combination of nature and nurture. As the weeks rolled on, more meetings, more hope, more truth, more identification.

'Look for the similarities, not the differences.' We were told.

Our egos and our competitive natures made judgment a second nature.

As the weeks went on I have no doubt I became 'enlightened'. The light was switched on. You see, if you want to see light, true light, then look into the eyes of a child. Radiance, truth, creativity instinct, self. As the death of my former self gained momentum, meditation, writing, step work, meetings, exercise, no escapism, and the real me started to return. The six year old Drewe.

Who was I? I was beginning to find out...

That year after Sporting Chance was tough but, profound.

September 2012 to September 2013 was full of more pain but, the universe was realigning me.

Ron passed away. My grandfather passed away. I moved out of the marital home. I worked hard on my emotional recovery. Weekly therapy 1:1. I sat in twelve step meetings. I worked through the steps. I was growing. The layers that had blocked me were being replaced by self-respect, self-worth, built on the back of rigorous honesty. I had two different "sponsors" in the fellowship of recovery. "Sponsors" were there to guide me. They were men and women who had walked down this road and were a little further ahead. I grew new friends. I had entered the world of the spirit.

The process of re discovering the lost self was well under way.

The most gruelling part yet, the most profound and liberating process I have ever seen and I have had A LOT of psychologists and therapists, was step 4.

"A fearless and moral inventory"

For six months I sat and wrote every:

Resentment

Fear

Harm to another

Sexual harms

I had ever had, or committed.

Looking at where I was: selfish, self-seeking, dishonest and fearful.

A reboot to my overloaded hard drive and dysfunctional system.

A brutal brutal process but, without it, a true re discovery of the lost self for me is impossible. It's my hope that one day this process is adopted by the FA and other governing boards of coach education. Without it potentially talented coaches will never be able to "unlock" that most vital component. Who they really are and why they act how they act and their part in their words and behaviours impact that impact others.

Over the six years between walking into Sporting Chance and writing this book so much has happened.

I have built and ended businesses.

I have worked with some of the nation's most talented athletes male and female.

I have mentored and guided CEOs and business leaders.

I got re married in September 2017 and am due to be a father again in April 2019.

I have guided and given my all to my daughter Talia. I have had such pleasure with the new feelings I feel and live in. The intense love. The fear. The compassion, the overwhelming empathy.

I own them all.

It was the Buddha that said "Life is suffering" yes it is.

To truly live is to feel to truly feel. Pain. Joy. Love and all the other emotions and feelings life presents.

Chapter 4- And Then What

Once you have it all. All you dreamed of. And Then What..?
Life and success , Is a daily manifestation of following our
visions and instincts.

And Then What...?

'And then what'; thank you to my beautiful wife, Helen, for giving me the title. I was sat at my desk on a Friday evening in December and had just ended a phone call with a young footballer whom I was mentoring.

'Why did you say and then what... about 10 times?' She asked.

The call started by him saying 'I'm only on eight goals and I need to be on ten by...'

'But why?' I asked.

'Because then I'll be in double figures and the clubs who are watching will probably sign me.'

'Oh, and then what?' I asked.

'What do you mean?'

'Well...' I said, 'what happens then?'

'I'll be a championship player. That's where I need to be because it's another step nearer to where I want to be; the Premier League.'

'And then what?' I asked.

'I don't know what you mean.' He sounded confused.

'Well, what happens when you get to the Premier League?'

'Then I want to be one of the best players there and play for my country...'

'Oh, oh,' I interrupted. 'Then you'll retire and have your cars and your houses and your millions of pounds and you'll holiday in amazing places and your kids will go to the best schools and you would've done it.'

He went a little quiet. 'I'm still not sure I know what you mean.' He said.

'What I mean is that what you think is your goal and your dream won't satisfy you because it's never ending. If I earn more, win more, if I get this car, or this house, if my kids could go to this school, if we could go on holiday to a hot place; if, if, if, if, if. It's so exhausting.' I said.

I went on, 'no wonder when I first saw you play 11 months ago you looked like you could hardly run, you were running around pulling a ten tonne truck full of crap. How many games has it been without you scoring a goal?'

'Five.' He said, 'and it's such an important time. The transfer window opens in two weeks.'

I asked him if I could make a suggestion, he said yes.

'Let go. Let go of all of it. You're trying to control it all, the whole thing. You're trying to force playing well and trying to think you can guarantee a great game. And, because of fears you're failing.'

He talked about a need to be better, to score, to not fail, to which I replied simply '…and then what?' We both laughed.

'Look mate,' I started, 'I'm not trying to kill you here, it's the opposite. I'm trying to show you that I have to live with the pain that I never fulfilled my potential as a player because of these fears that are currently ruling you.'

There are some simple questions that this footballer and, in fact, anybody, can answer; who are you? What do you love to do? What are you good at? Answering these truths is all you have to do.

I said, 'You're a great athlete, you're a strong runner, you're big, powerful. You time your runs so naturally. Just stop with this rubbish and be you. If you do, I promise you that it will just happen. Your dreams and goals are just a vision into your future. It's going to happen but not if you try to control it because of fear. Tomorrow, be you. Have a laugh with the boys in the dressing room, go for a warm up run, pass sharply, set your head ready for 90 minutes of brutal hard work. Run, run, run and when your body is screaming for you to stop, run again.'

This was followed by a big sigh. 'That ok mate?' I asked.

'Yeah.' He said. 'Thank you. I feel so clear now, like everything has lifted.'

The reason was purely because his fear was mind made and based on completely made up thoughts that had stacked up in his head.

'I just lifted them up, like a crane, and dumped them in the bin.' I said, after my explanation. 'Now go and chill and we'll speak tomorrow.'

He scored two goals the next day and led his side to a 2-1 victory. Now, let me elaborate on the meaning of this story I've just shared with you. It's my belief that we all come into this world completely free of fear and conditioning. When we're born, we go into a system that is already in place; a family system, then onto an education system, perhaps during that time you're part of a club, which has a separate system.

Whether that club is a football team, a reading group or a squash club, it will have a different set of teachers and leaders operating in it.

Unless the teachers and leaders you meet throughout your life are all very emotionally aware and aware of their own frailties, you might find, and what I have found, is that they project their stuff, their baggage, onto you.

Those projections will make us doubt ourselves. That doubt of ourselves causes a splitting from our 'naturalness'. When you're a toddler, you're completely natural. Toddlers find their way in the world with touch, feel and senses. When they need to eat or sleep, they let you know.

And then the conditioning begins. This is what the story I shared with you at the beginning of this chapter is all about. The young man who I speak about never doubted himself as a young player, he just did what he did; he was what he was.

Him being him slowly made him become the best footballer in his school, then in the next club, and in the next club. Then, he was signed by one of the biggest footballing academies in the country.

That's when the splitting started. He started to split from who he truly was and started to search for something that he already had inside him. That is where the pattern of asking 'and then what?' reemerged.

This doubt had made him question where he was going and how he could get there. He started 'the search' and the truth is, all he was searching for was already there. My search started when I was about 10 years old.

Are you searching now?

I'd suggest that if you are thinking you need to get somewhere, then really the journey you need to take is the journey back to self. That is really what I believe life is; and we're all on that journey.

The people who are completely aligned with who they are don't just soar through life. Of course, life will do what it does; illness, death, loss, grief, sadness and happiness are just some of the inevitabilities. What life brings is going to happen anyway and that should be acknowledged. But, if it's going to happen anyway, there's nothing to stop you from being aligned in the here and now.

We've had influences from very early on and we become emotionally aware from a young age as a result of our parents and the first teachers who have guided and guided.

For me, Tiger Woods is a great example. He soared from a young boy. His chosen path was golf, although some would say it was chosen for him. He soared through local tournaments, international tournaments and before long he was a professional winning tournaments. He dominated golf for 20 years and changed the whole landscape of the game.

What is very fascinating, and what became clear when listening to his interviews, is that in more recent years he has started to split from himself. Woods' Dad was a very prominent figure in his life; he regularly talks about how he treated him as an equal. There are pictures of Woods from around the age of six and his Dad is always sitting on the floor, talking to him at eye level; treating him as an equal.

Interviews with him speak about the tournament at Augusta when Woods knew his father didn't have long left to live. He put too much pressure on himself in that tournament and found himself nowhere near the winning post. He talks then about how, in some of the last words Woods had with his father, his Dad said, 'don't ever do that again, son; don't ever play for anybody else; me, them, sponsors - always for yourself.'

Woods embraced that attitude and lived in that place for many, many years. He was brought up a Buddhist with a strong Mother teaching that belief to him. The teachings include attachment to nothing, alignment with oneself and to be still. Woods was still. He soared through the world of golf and changed the very nature of the sport, probably forever.

As he went on life became harder. He got to the top and all of a sudden there are questions, sponsors, pressure, TV, more views, social media, people trying to change who you are, more people saying do it this way, do it that way. To add to that, the self-critic starts to creep in. For a natural competitor like Woods, that voice would always be there, on his shoulder.

I've got be better, I've got to be sharper, they're after you, look at him, look at his score, got to shoot lower, got to go to the gym, got to work harder, need to practice more. The tragic truth is, and this is something that I - and a lot of other people - can relate to; that it's hard to stop self-doubt from creeping in. To stop that niggling feeling that you need to 'be more' than yourself. The gift is the curse. The gift of fierce competitiveness constantly battering him, more , more ,more.

Woods thought he needed to do more to stay ahead. But, what did he do to get ahead? He worked hard, of course, but when he was 12, 13, 14, 15 he wasn't getting up at 4am to train. Then, all of a sudden into his 20s there are stories emerging of him training with the Navy Seals and lifting weights at 3am. He began searching. Yes, wake up early, get on the range, practice, but don't ever try to be crazy about it. Don't ever try to be more than yourself because that search will destroy you.

That search destroyed me and I think it destroys a lot of people. Be yourself, there is no 'and then what?', there is no finish line. There is only who you are. And between Zero or Eighty, or however long you live, throughout your life journey you will pick up accolades. Your achievement might be to be a great Mother, have gifts of empathy and care, become an exceptional Nurse. But, do you want or need to become the best Nurse in the world? Well, you might get there. People might acknowledge us and think we're the best in the world. Yes, that's fantastic, but follow your voice and it will lead you where you need to go.

Your voice might tell you to go to work early and finish late or do the extra thing. That's who you are, but don't look for more.

Over the chapters that follow, I'm hopefully going to break down all of the permutations of this, from self-belief to ego to the illusion of needs. So, let's go on this journey together.

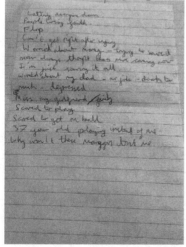

An exercise I get my clients to do weekly is Fear and Resentment Inventories. To strip their Heart of all the blocks to themselves and their potential

Chapter 5 - Self Belief

You have got to know what it is you want, or someone is going to sell you a bill of goods somewhere along the line that can do irreparable damage to your self-esteem, your sense of worth, and your stewardship of the talents that God gave you.

—Richard Nelson Bolles

And Then What...?

The 25th July 2007 at 6.30pm is a day I'll never forget.

It was one of those hot July days. I used to hate evening matches; I had all day to sit and think. Every second would tick over in my mind and with every thought, a powerful emotion would follow.

'You need to make sure you do this.' 'Are you good enough?' 'You have to remember to play well.' 'Ok, so, what do you need to do to play well?' 'Yes, but can I do that? Am I capable of that?' 'You need to step up, Drewe.' I would toss and turn as I was sleeping, if I went for a walk I couldn't get rid of the constant over-analysis. The chatter was relentless.

The tragedy, looking back, and what I still have to work hard to accept now, is that it didn't have to be that way.

On that day, I was last in through the dressing room door. I walked across the room, took my shirt off - which was covered in sweat. I slumped onto my seat and dropped my head down. My heart rate was up at 185bpm.

It was quiet; that horrible mixture of tiredness, fear and dissection. The door swung open.

'What was that?'

I could hear sentences like 'second to the ball' 'overlapping' 'caught in possession' as I zoned in and out. 'What are you doing? Are you listening, Drewe?' I looked up.

'You give the ball away, you haven't won a header, and you offer nothing. You've got 10 minutes and you're coming off.'

The rest was a bit of a blur.

That was Paul Ince; a man I admired greatly. He had a presence. He had fought the fight and knew what it took, he really knew.

This was his first real managerial role having taken a short term roll at Macclesfield Town, where he achieved an amazing feat by keeping them safe after inheriting a lost cause.

He had asked me to come in to play two games, show I'm fit and then he would sign me. It was the end of July; two weeks to the new season.

I didn't just want this opportunity, I *needed* it. I wanted it badly. I was back home after years of travelling. I was in a nice stadium with good players and finally a better team to be a part of.

The door swung open again and out he walked. My mind and body was a cocktail of fear, anxiety, naiveness and fatigue.

I got up and walked to the toilet area, pulled open a cubicle and sat on the seat. I closed the door and sat, desperately trying to find a solution and work out what had gone on.

'You're finished.' A voice in my head said. 'You have no contract. You're playing for your future. It's over.'

'You let him beat you for the first goal.' '10 minutes and you're off.' 'Your family are here.'

That voice had beaten me more times than I had beaten it over the 12 years I had been a professional.

There was silence. 'Two minutes, boys.' The assistant manager shouted. It was silent once more.

'What are you doing?' An empathetic yet decisive voice echoed around my soul. 'You're trying to fit in, look good in your nice, white kit. You're in your nice stadium playing against top internationals. *What are you doing?*' 'Premier league, no premier league they are just guys. Some technically gifted, some honest, some hard working but, fucking hell come on don't buy into names and reputations , please'

'This isn't you.' The voice continued. 'Last season you learned to fight the opposition in a stadium a tenth of this size. You fought, you showed no respect. GET UP AND BE YOU.'

My head lifted. I smiled and pushed the door open.

The buzzer sounded; that was the trigger for us to be back in the tunnel for the second half.

I walked to the sink, splashed my face with water and looked hard at myself. 'If I'm going down, I'm not going down like this. I'm doing me.' I said to myself.

I pulled one of the players to the side. 'Mate, I'm not going to show at little angles, it's killing me. It's too congested. Hit me long, hang the first few up, let me see if they fancy it.'

The whistle blew 30 seconds later. I saw the player I'd spoken with, with the ball at his feet, looking up. I pulled away. He hung the ball up. I jumped early; I was so good in the air, effortless.

'Bang'. I headed the ball 20 yards to the winger. As I did, my elbow clattered into the defender. It was clean, but he went down. I left him and ran into position.

The next 45 minutes went so quickly. I won nearly every header , held the ball up, won a penalty and made another goal. It was one of those beautiful, beautiful moments you want to live in forever. The time when you're doing you, fearlessly and with courage and it's all effortless.

I got a contract and much praise and admiration after that performance. Sadly, it wasn't long before self-doubt got me again and the season petered out with only fleeting moments of that Drewe.

Tangling with West Ham and Welsh defender Danny gabbidon during the match

The truth is, I didn't know how that performance happened. I couldn't possibly recreate 'it' when I didn't know what 'it' was.

Now I look back, what 'it' was, was me. Myself.

The first half I doubted and then lost my self.

In that dressing room at half time my soul stirred. It wasn't my destiny to go down that night; that time would come five years later.

I found myself for 45 minutes in that game. I actually momentarily believe in myself. I had… self-belief!

'Just believe in yourself.' How many times have I heard those four simple words? The sentence is treated as if just by it pushing through somebody's vocal chords and out through their lips it would instantly give the recipient what it promises.

So often, the person uttering these four words rarely knew what they meant. What's even more grave is that the same person rarely had 'it' themselves.

Of course, the 'it' I'm talking about is self-belief.

To really understand this sentence we must understand the two words individually.

Self. The Self. Our Self. What does it mean to you? It's not easy to answer.

For me, the story that I began this chapter with is the best example of self-belief I have. There I was, sitting in the toilet cubicle, riddled by fear. I was virtually paralysed by what seemed like a guaranteed realisation that I was finished. My career would be done, I'd be ridiculed and pitied and I'd have to sit through those 'it'll be ok' conversations.

For 45 little minutes, 2,700 seconds, I had committed the most tragic and the most serious of crimes. I had let self-doubt beat self-belief. Sat in that cubicle I had two, maybe three, minutes to 'find something'.

If we lose our car keys we look under cushions, pull out drawers, shout, open the dustbin. It's crazy really; the panic that ensues.

Yet, there I was, a certain outcome inevitable, circling me like vultures waiting for the kill. Where could I possibly look for answers?

As I sat and let that internal stream of conversation and relentless confirmation of doubt flow, my true self finally stood up, gingerly, scared by this big, aggressive bully called doubt.

It whispered so softly, 'That's not you, can you hear me, my friend? That's not you.' It was almost pleading; 'Follow me. Please get up and follow me. Don't be scared.'

It takes a lot of courage to be faithful to self-belief. To trust it, but ultimately it's the truth. It's the truth because it's in you.

Who are you without all of these doubts? These mind-made, fear-based doubts. You, that child who would go first, would put your hand up first, who would run harder when hurting during cross country.

You are a leader, you are strong, you are brave, you are sensitive, you are kind, you have a great moral fibre.

Now, get up and be you.

Now I knew going into that evening that there was no formality to proceedings. A contract wasn't just waiting despite what had been said 'just play in these two games and we will get a contract all sorted'. Luckily I had been around long enough to know there were no handouts. I was on trial. There was doubt. I had to play well. I had to show them I was worthy not just of a contract but a good one.

That mix of fear and anxiety yet focus and excitement, too. Looking back as a retired player it's this mix of emotions and that cocktail of feelings that I miss so much. With too much of the wrong fear you go under. With not enough of the right fear you don't have the edge. I had the wrong fears too many times in my life. I say 'wrong fears' but I suppose you're wondering what I mean by that. It's fear that's completely and utterly out of my control and fears that I'm completely powerless over. Will I play well? Am I good enough? Is he better/stronger/quicker than me? Will I fail? Do they like me? Will I get a contract? Am I crap?

On the best days of my career I had surrendered. I'd surrendered to my mind, surrendered to my thoughts and accepted my utter powerlessness in controlling anything. Knowing all I had was me; flesh, blood, spirit. So I aligned my spirit, which was letting go of all my thoughts, with my physique, to run, to push, to sweat, to fight. To just be.

At 29, my soul, my being, was buried. I had violated it, lied to it, been unfaithful to it, crossed it and mocked it so many times that it was nearly lost. I am so grateful to say 'nearly', there.

My soul will never leave me and neither will yours.

Today, I listen to it, I'm led by it, I ask it for guidance and for help. It's not easy, but it's meant to be. It's the struggle that creates character and the character that changes things, that leads and that innovates. It takes great courage to back ourselves.

But, what choice do we really have other than to back ourselves? I say none. It will make us sick, it will give us headaches and it won't leave us. How can it leave us? It is us.

I heard from a Doctor friend recently that when they know someone is struggling with symptoms that are stress related they just label it IBS! When we feel anxiety and fear we feel it in our guts. When we have "heart ache" where do we feel it? In our guts. When we feel the love from a hug or cuddle it's ... in our guts. How many physical diseases are caused by emotional Illness , spiritual sickness, identification with thoughts and our heads? Many I think.

John Bradshaw a famous psychotherapist, who's work can be found still via any one of his books or his Television series on You Tube. After 30 years in clinic he went to the hospital a few blocks away and sat with the head of the cancer department. They collaborated patient notes over a period of time and the findings were, I believe in right in saying, profound. So many of Bradshaw patients who were addicts, co dependents, spiritually bankrupt, emotionally abused, emotional trauma clients had been to the hospital with cancers. I'm in no way saying that ALL illnesses are caused by this but I have a huge belief that when we stray from our path, WHO we are it will manifest in a number of physical Symptoms.

That is what 'self' is after all. I say, don't believe in it, just trust it.

To believe in oneself. Well, who is oneself? This story is a perfect example. I found myself sitting, at 8.40pm, in a toilet cubicle in the bowels of a football stadium. I was in silence. Five minutes from a brutal reality. A still quiet voice whispered, 'Just try being you…'

My life, all aspects of it, to that point, was a series of brilliant highs and crushing lows; a polarity which I was so tired of. Anybody who can relate to this will understand. The moments you are finally yourself in thought, words and deed. At a family BBQ, with friends, in the workplace, when participating in a hobby. A calmness descends; a serenity. All outcomes disappear and scenarios evaporate. Whether you're with a partner or children, and truly in that moment. Whether you're playing recreational golf or tennis and you surprise yourself with how good you actually are. To be yourself is to be completely authentic. So why's it so hard to maintain or find? What even is it you're trying to find? How does it get lost in the first place?

There is, of course, the classic theories of the split occurring at childhood, when emotional needs aren't met. Picture the Victorian parents and the requisite at the time of being seen and not heard. As a result of this, a child believes he/she can't be themselves. Their unformed conscience might say 'bang the drum' 'play with the toys' 'scream' 'make a den' 'play chase' - all of these are instinctive childlike reactions. Quickly, though, the natural state is shamed. Seen and not heard translates to a child as don't be yourself or do what you want to do instinctively and creatively.

Without a doubt, this is a huge thing and so is the work done by brilliant therapists over the years on toxic shame. Healthy shame might be something like me saying to my daughter 'Honey, shut the door when you're on the toilet, please.' Yes, she's embarrassed that somebody has seen her naked and exposed but it's how she learns some society-based rights from wrongs.

Toxic shame would be to say 'You're disgusting. Who goes to the toilet with the door open? That disgusts me.'

The 'you are' statements and being called disgusting as a human being for a behaviour you have no awareness over. If I said that to her, she thinks in that moment that she is disgusting. What sort of human must I be if I do that? Will be the types of thoughts flowing through her brain. As a result, the 'it's not ok to be me' mindset begins.

So, if it's not ok to be me, who can I be? Ah, the ego. The mind-made false sense of self. The self in which we must believe in is that instinct and that gut feeling. But we live in a world that will make us second guess ourselves on such a scale, as many others who are lost project their opinions upon us. Trauma and abuse will also create that loss of self.

How about for those who don't have the toxic shame or abuse? Those like me who have an inner critic so huge that the battle will be with my own shadow my whole life. I spent eight years in therapy, I've looked at my childhood, my inner child, shame and escapism, addiction and loss of self. Today I am as closely aligned to my true state as I ever have been. Today I'll be pulled very quickly into doubt; the hyenas cackling; who are you kidding? You're shit. You can't write a good book, you're not a good Dad - look at you, you're fat. All those inner critics will start very quickly.

Today, I truly believe that those were the gifts of huge competitiveness or the calling to really make a dent in the world. It's not a case of better or worse than, it's just what it is for me. For me, those voices negatively are as loud as those voices positively. Iris absolutely owning your demons. Your shadow side. It's Freudian. Today I can own that I have a voice and edge so ruthless you just wouldn't want to be near that side of me daily but, it's absolutely gold dust for getting a job done. Giving motivation and strength and courage to others. In the same soul I have a caring nature and compassion so huge I can just cuddle puppies and smother my family with kisses. I say to clients today unless you can own your darkness you'll never fully walk in your light.

And Then What...?

When the real me shows up, I'm blessed with the capabilities to achieve amazing feats quickly - very quickly. If the ego, fear-based false-me turns up, that person has the capabilities to alienate myself very quickly and be an absolute shadow of my true self. This Jekyll and Hyde character is part of my makeup, both extremely powerful. If the real me shows up and achieves the feats quickly, I get notoriety and praise but, then the shadow side shows up again and skews my vision; you're better than all of them, you don't need them, you're great, you don't need anyone.

Chapter 6- Ego, The Silent Killer

We didn't necessarily like ourselves or want to be so self-centered. But we had no inner resources to help us escape the trap of our egos. When we were there, we could not see outside ourselves well enough to ask for help. Surrender, we thought, brought only defeat and humiliation.

And Then What...?

It was a scorching hot July day, only 9am but already 26 degrees. I sat on the bonnet of my car in a lay-by down a quiet country road. I hadn't slept for days and my weary eyes were hidden behind my dark aviators. I started to drift off as the power of the sun permeated the glass and made my eyes squint. I was snapped out of it as the sound of a diesel engine came round the corner; Ron's black Vauxhall, unmistakable.

He pulled up behind me. I didn't look round as I heard his car door open. I could hear the sound of his feet walking around the car to where I was, sat on the bonnet. I got up. I was almost dizzy with tiredness and the morning sun.

'Hi mate.' He said.

'Hi Ron.'

'You're lucky, I'm working from home this morning but I've got to be in London this afternoon. So, what's going on?'

'I'm so, so scared. I haven't slept in days. The season's two weeks away. I put so much pressure on myself in the trials I've had so far that I didn't perform. I just don't know how to keep doing this, Ron. I'm 29 now. I haven't got it in me to keep going. It was a year ago this month that I was at Milton Keynes in the same situation, on trial. That Chelsea game, that West Ham game, I found it. And here I am a year later.' I started to sob again.

It was the outpouring of a thousand emotions of fear. All my feelings and doubts poured from me.

'Oh Drewe.' Ron said to me as he walked up to me and put a hand on my shoulder.

After a few minutes there was no more pent up feelings to outpour. I was done.

I stepped away and said, 'I just can't do it anymore.'

'I know.' Ron said, 'but something will come. There will be an opportunity, trust me. Look, I've got to go. You should go home, you need to keep believing. What are you doing today?'

'I'm going to go and workout again. I'm going to run. Do some hill runs.'

'Go and do that. Let's speak later.'

As the back of his black Vauxhall disappeared around the corner I took a deep breath. I got into my car, put the key in the ignition and drove away. I didn't put the radio on. I sat in silence with a mixture of relief and surrender. There was a complete stillness in the car and after weeks and weeks, my head felt it, too.

The phone rang. A name I was always comforted by appeared on the screen. But today, I didn't need any comfort. All was well; I was in a completely carefree place.

'Hi mate.' Said a familiar voice.

'Hey.' I replied.

'I don't know how to start this...' He said.

'Go on. It's fine, just say what you need to say.'

One week into the new football season and I hadn't had many offers. Unsurprising, as I'd barely played the previous season. I'd had a terrible twelve weeks since the end of the previous season. Fear had overwhelmed me. Trials, rejections, self-doubt and tears; and through it all my ego had been slowly smashed to pieces.

I had already had a trial at Rotherham United. It was full of pressure and my mind was living in a world of worst case scenarios. I had huffed and puffed my way through 90 minutes against Scunthorpe United.

They chose not to sign me that night. Instead, manager Mark Robins, signed a young athlete, Ruben Reid, who went on to have a wonderful season. Ironically, as my strike partner.

On August 5th the phone rang:

'Drewe, its Mark Robins.'

'Hi Mark.'

'Have you got a club yet?'

'No.' I said.

'Look, come up here. I can't get my number one target for eight weeks, so come and train and we will see if we can offer you something.'

I drove up that Tuesday morning in August. I felt beaten. My ego crushed. I had surrendered. Surrendered to life, to football. To my need to control and control and try to steer myself towards my goals.

I trained Tuesday, Wednesday and Thursday. I just played; I *just* ran. I just helped a mate out who needed me to bail him out. I sweated. I pushed. I laughed; yes, I laughed!

Laughter and me have always had a strange relationship. The true Drewe is a funny guy. He's the kind of guy who would always be centre of the party. I always had that ability, on and off the pitch.

'You'll be on a 4 week contract at £250 a week.' Ron said.

'Amazing.' I said.

They were actually going to pay me money to play this wonderful game and keep fit?

'Drewe, £250 a week. That's an eighth of what you earned last year.'

'Yeah, I know. I hope you told them yes and I can't wait.' I replied.

Ron knew me by now. The unpredictability, the zero to hero, the creative gifts and the self-destruct button; all in one body, no less. I must say, though, even he was shocked at my response.

Over the four weeks that followed I found the place that I had found many times in the 12 years as a professional that had preceded this point. When I woke without my alarm, when I woke with anticipation not dread. Excitement not fear. Living was amazing.

'Is this what it's like to be alive?' I remember thinking.

2003 was another occasion. I was a player at Southend United at the time. I had endured such low, low times. I sat alone in my apartment, my BMW outside. On the surface everything looked good but my soul was in turmoil. My head awash with thoughts. I was signed by Steve Wignall at the start of an ill-fated, yet powerful, season in the club's history.

I was completely devoid of all form and belief by November. I was in the reserves, playing on cold Tuesday nights to no crowd. The team was made of players retiring from injury, young hopefuls looking for a break and senior first team players lacking form.

Lost and confused, I would call it. During that period Steve Tilson took the reserves. He was an ex player and a club legend. Steve was a good man. I liked playing for him. His demands were simple; work hard and run. The meetings, the focus on opposition and the fear mongering wasn't present.

I started to play well, score a few goals and get some semblance of belief back. In December after some poor results, Steve got the first team job. I wasn't an immediate starter but had thrown away the perfectionist attitude that had sabotaged most of my career to date. I had worked really hard and just 'mucked in'. You see, to a guy wired like I am, that's a tough concept to accept. That just by being part of a cause and working hard you can maximize your potential. I got into Southend's team coinciding with the teams run in a league cup competition. I scored goals at will against Luton, QPR and famously Colchester United. We faced the local rivals over two legs of a semifinal. I scored home and away. The equalising goal.

Me in action for Southend United during one of the best spells of my career. Again I had found the elusive "it"

At a packed Roots Hall Stadium, I helped the club to the first final in the club's history. I was on fire. Ironically whilst in Sporting Chance, founder and ex Arsenal and England captain, Tony Adams, came to talk to us about his struggles. We sat having a coffee and he shared with me that he had been sent to watch me by a top championship club. I was in the fourth division. They were in the second and on their way to the top league.

'You were on fire. Scoring goals, leading, fit, strong, a real player then all of a sudden, nothing! You weren't playing and out the team?'

'Story of my life, Tony.' I said. 'As soon as i started doing well a voice would start up. You can't keep this up! You're blagging it! It's not this simple.'

'Wow.' He said. 'Yeah, we never signed you, the manager said to much of a risk.'

Back to Rotherham 2007.

I played some of the best football of my career. I scored five goals, I led the line, I played fearlessly and with the absence of anything other than my God given soul. I was the leader I always was.

People were shocked at the levels I was playing at. I became central to Rotherham's incredible season. We beat Leeds United, Leicester city, Wolves, Sheffield Wednesday and ran Stoke City close on an amazing cup run. I was scoring and leading the line. Keep in mind we started the season minus 15 points due to financial mismanagement of the club.

Bournemouth, led by Eddie Howe and now flying high in The Premier League also began minus fifteen points. I didn't know it again but, I had surrendered. I had been dragged through so much pain that summer a year on from exactly the scenario at Mk Dons FC that I just accepted my utter powerlessness over EVERYTHING other than the ability to run and fight. If insanity was doing the same thing and expecting a different result then without doubt, I was insane!

The £250 contract was renewed and I was given a deal more in line with my market value in just four weeks.

Me in action during an amazing run of form against the odds at Rotherham United.

Now, here's the tragedy; it lasted ten weeks at best. As I started to get headlines and notoriety again, as the glory and admiration poured in. The voice that I thought was dead, a voice I thought I had *finally* defeated, started to whisper. The whispers turned to calling and the calling turned to deafening shouting.

'Who are you kidding? No pressure, but you think you can keep this up? You think it's that easy? You can train and have a laugh with your teammates, but if you want to get to the top, you're going to need to do more.' My ego screamed at me.

There was one morning at training when I was out of the starting team. I had caused that by my levels dropping through too much pressure again. It was the day before training and we were involved in what is a very standard and customary session at all clubs worldwide at ALL levels of the game. An 11v11. Basically the starting 11 (the 11 players the manager has picked for the game the following day) play against the remaining players.

65

I used to be great here. Why? Anger. 'I will show' them this little voice would say. On this one particular morning I was in that place. We were beating the 'first team' and I was on fire. Bullying the players and making things happen.

'Stop, stop' Shouted the manager.

'I'm going to change a few things. Drewe swap bibs with Richie' Now Richie was and is a lovely guy. Was a player who had a great career. A real tough Yorkshire man. But I was in that zone. The wounded me was rampant , the fighter provoked.

As Richie and I walked towards each other from one end of the pitch to the other to swap shirts I grabbed his shirt and said 'give me that, I will show you how shit gets done' I cringe as I write that today. I am really sorry Rich . You must understand the wounded beast in me I didn't know how to control and the real tragedy is that I thought that, that is where my best performances come from. Anger and 'proving people wrong' what a mythical thing.

Anger runs out. Truth is full of energy. Acceptance. I'm not playing because the managers job is on the line and the last two weeks my fork has been poor. I think the hardest thing for players "wired" like me is that ALL we crave is an arm around us. Again to be asked 'Are you ok Drewe'? 'What's going on'? ' how can we get you back to the player we know is in there'? In all my years and speaking to senior guys today and in the corporate world, that is still NOT happening. So it's fight or flight mode constantly.

Do more. Two words that have plagued my life. 'Nothing is enough' are three more.

You see, my ego had been destroyed because it was built on exterior things; identity as a player, car, money, etc.

Now, I was stripped back and my creative source was back at my core. I rose quickly, I always did. But, the curse of a gift, a destiny or a calling is that I believe on our deepest level we know what we're capable of. And, we won't rest until we achieve it.

I was en route. I was being my natural self, achieving and getting glory. That deep part of me got excited. 'You're back.' 'You're on track.' 'Come on, you have to do it this time.' It said.

The tragedy is, I couldn't understand back then that I was en route only because I had surrendered to my powerlessness to control.

I'm better than you. I look down on you. I will smile at you but deep down I'm twice the person you are. I can't possibly be seen with him/them; what would people think of me? I need to be seen as elite, not average or normal. Just look what they're wearing.

Please tell me I'm the best. Tell me how wonderful I am; that you can't live without me, that I'm irreplaceable.

These are some of the many thoughts that have led and defined me for the best part of 23 years of my life. Between the ages of 10 and 33 that's who I was, or at least, I thought that was the case.

Ego is a word that, just like self-belief, is bandied about so readily. In my experience, it's said without any understanding of its meaning or origin; 'He has got a big ego,' people will say. Other comments like: 'They are a team of big egos, it will take some managing,' are commonplace.

The truth is, ego was a slow and silent killer for me. It was so misunderstood, so undetected it drove me and consistently sabotaged my true potential, who I actually was and what I was capable of.

We don't know who we are because it's so buried and lost. We are who we tell ourselves at our core we are but ultimately, at our core is our ego.

I had 22 employers in 17 years. That's not impressive in the least. Ok, 22 people thought I was good, but it's a desperate state of affairs; I lived my life flat to flat, always on the move. I was always reaching to prove a point and ready to rub the previous employers' noses in it. Who was wrong? Them? At the time, yes. How could they do this to me? I'd think. Can't they see how good I am?

Ego, ego, ego.

'A mind made false sense of self.'

I want you to slowly reflect on this quote 5-10 times. Analyse it word by word. It's the best definition I have ever found or heard.

The reason this chapter follows on from self-belief is because as you look to discover the real you, your self-belief can get lost and an ego can develop. If you've lived a happy life, particularly childhood, your needs would've been met. Your emotional needs will be met and you'll be loved by people unconditionally.

The ego normally develops a little later on, as you learn more, see more, experience more; it will help to shape your true self.

Ego will trick you. It is to the soul what cancer is to the body. It will grow. It will make you sick and drain you of energy. It will trick others but more importantly, you'll be tricking yourself.

I'm going to take you back to me and my life; there's good reason, I promise! As I said, I had 22 employers in 17 years. My natural self was ambitious, super-competitive, expected high standards, empathetic, caring and passionate. These are all incredible qualities to be blessed with. Many of these qualities held up as the qualities of a leader. At my source, that's who I am; a leader.

I had a mentor who came into my life when I was 21. His name was Ron Alfred. This book wouldn't be a true reflection of my life if I didn't talk about Ron. I think of him a lot. Ron passed in the summer of 2013. He died from leukaemia.

I met Ron when I was eight. I was playing for my local Sunday team, Woburn Lions FC. Ron's two sons both played, too; both were talented players. I didn't see Ron again until my 21st birthday party, a surprise arranged by my brother, Gregg.

Me aged 12 with Norwich City back row second from right next to Rons son Ricky who was really talented and a lovely human being. With Woburn Lions my Sunday team in 1988. It was here I met Ron and his sons Ricky and Chris.

I was struggling at the time. I was at such a critical age. I hadn't established myself and was very close to sliding down a cliff face to footballing oblivion.

'If you ever need to talk, I'm here mate.' Ron said. I called him three days later. That started our relationship, which lasted 10 years until I was 31.

Ron had a gift to see people's true potential. He saw mine.

For 10 years we shared many great moments; Saturday afternoons, Tuesday nights - I'd be the true Drewe by the time he showed up. We believed anything was possible and held onto these moments.

The greatest testament to Ron is that he saw 'me'. He saw through the fear, through the insecurities masquerading as strength. Through the clothes, the image and the pretense, he saw me.

We battled courageously together for all of those ten years. The fight was never against an opponent however big they were in stature or reputation. We fought my ego; my mind made sense of who I am.

The times I was 'me' (the 'me' he saw all along) were infrequent and relative to the amount of times I exhibited my talent in public. Usually, I stumbled across 'me' when I was at the bottom. Being at the bottom, written off, doubted, pigeonholed, without any rights, against all odds, stripped of glory, stripped of reputation; that's when I was left with nothing more than 'me'.

In those dark hours, the natural response, the internal dialogue, was always the same: 'Let's get going now.' An almost masochistic voice would say; a voice that enjoyed being taken to the brink and being completely written off.

You see, the ego is the most deadly and sad of things. Like bars around a prison cell, it locks up true self, the true you, the true me… and throws away the key.

This book, my writings, are all so linked. From self-belief to ego, to leadership and the illusion of needs. At 33 years of age there was nothing left for my ego to cling to. The ego feeds off of anything that lies outside of ourselves. It's like a cancer feeding from the body and the only way to cut the supply us a brutal pummelling. Chemotherapy is like dropping a nuclear bomb into our bodies; it decimates everything in its path leaving the spirit and the organs to fight back. It strips us, and all that we have, back physically.

The ego needs a different type of pummelling. It needs all extras and materialism stripped away. The 'title', the money, the car, the job, the glory; so that all you are left with is you.

And Then What...?

Winston Churchill is a man I greatly admire and have studied and read much on.

There's a line he once used when writing one of his greatest speeches of all time at the time of the D Day Landings.

'Fighting is what I've always done. It's the core of who I am.'

'Who will I be when it's all over? What will I be like, When I'm done fighting.' ?

In the research I've done, I feel like Churchill was a man with great gifts. At times, his ego held him prisoner and glory became his focus. But, in the most part, and what is really humbling, is that he remembered who he was and what he was.

I would suggest he is heralded as the 'greatest ever Briton' because he aligned himself with his true self; his soul.

There has been, and will continue to be, many, many people who would clamber over one another to point out his faults. What I'm suggesting is that his faults arrived, like many of us, when his mind made sense of self outmuscled his true self.

The pain felt when the ego is running things is a pain I wouldn't wish on my worst enemy.

I'm going to go off on a tangent here; I'm currently sat on a plane. There's a couple in front with a 2-3 year old daughter; we're three hours into an 8 hour flight. The little girl has been asleep and quiet as a mouse so far. But, she has just woken up; she's tired and she's crying. I speak as a father of a 5-year-old little girl. The parents are saying 'be quiet', 'stop crying' and 'stop' to her. Most recently the said 'you're being embarrassing' to her. I really think they said this completely subconsciously, not thinking about the long-term ramifications.

In reality, the child is being her. She can't communicate properly yet, so when she's sad, she cries. She's bored and she wants to get off. On some levels, her brain will be slowly tallying up the times she has been told to be quiet. 'So, being me is embarrassing? But, they're my creators. This is my vision of the world right now and it's not acceptable to be me.'

I am, by no means, the perfect parent. Who is? I'm sure when I've been tired and fed up I've snapped at my baby girl and then gone on to deeply regret it later on. I've never said a sentence like 'you are embarrassing' though.

'You are' - two simple words that are so final. To the receiver, they are taken in as 'I am'.

'I am an embarrassment to my primary care givers, my vision of perfection.'

From the bottom of my heart, and I don't think I'm being extreme, I believe we all feel this shaming that is put upon us from so many different angles in life.

I think my gift is my sensitivity. I feel everything. Others may not feel like this on the level that I do, but I believe shame can seep really deep in all people.

Anyway, back to delving into my memory, before I was disturbed by the present potential formulation of ego in another soul.

If this little girl feels she's embarrassing, the next step is that she can't show her true feelings as she will be shamed. That, in turn, begins the formulation of a pretend self.

I'm not a scientist and it's important for me to reiterate that. There will be people and psychologists with many letters following their names who will 'prove' I'm wrong; whatever 'wrong' means and whoever the judge and the jury is? The truth is, I just know. My ego grew to protect me but if truth, it killed me.

Chapter 7- Who am I?

I am that knowing deep down. That feeling. That vision. I am that instinct . I am that effortless ease with which I can make stuff happen. I am not who others tell me I am. I am that I am .

And Then What...?

I was left with this question at 33, sitting in a cottage in the woods at the Sporting Chance Clinic for rehabilitation. I was in there for emotional damage and traumas that acted out as addictive tendencies.

Who I am? The young guy who at 8 years of age was so excited to play in the Swallowfield Schools' annual 6-a-side tournament every June. I hardly slept, I could picture the nets hanging from the goals, almost glowing they were that white.

I am the guy who was kept awake by my dreams that I would score so many goals. I'd imagine the feeling I'd have when the ball left my foot and flew past the goalkeeper in slow motion as he strained with all he had to reach it.

I am the guy who when my father used to pick us up on a Saturday morning to take us to his house for the weekend with his new girlfriend, I would immediately feel my mums pain as she stood despairingly at the end of the drive arms open, struggling to conceal her pain.

I am so sensitive. I feel at levels I know others don't. I lost count of the amount of times I opened my heart, pulled back the shutters and lifted the lid on my feelings.

The loneliness; my god the loneliness. Today I still get it. I'm a little more careful who I share my feelings with, I understand the power of that gift must be used in the right areas. I am the guy who would never take a dive in a match to con a referee despite the strict instructions from my manager and his coaching staff to do so.

I am the guy who just couldn't face myself if when doing running drills I didn't completely get to the cone. Whose value system and moral compass coupled with my sensitivity made it almost impossible at times to survive on this planet.

I am the guy who would get so crippled with anxiety pre-game that I wanted to vomit. Such was the pressure put on by my knowledge of what I HAD to go and do to satisfy the standards of this brutally ambitious spirit.

I am the guy who wrote poetry privately to express my feelings. I think of my work today as a performance coach; I don't particularly like that label but, I guess I need one. Really I am just a guy who life has taught some wisdoms to. I clear the crap, the buildup of debris and lead a client back to themselves. I walk away from the ones who aren't ready. There's no magic potion. At some point' they, you, I, we all did things by instincts. We were all children living in our feelings.

74

The question 'who am I?' I believe is one of the most profound questions any of us will ever ask ourselves. In the dead of night, sitting in that cottage in a small single bed in a room with nothing else but the bed and the wardrobe, I finally asked myself.

I stripped away the car, the career the identity, the money, the glory and the family. There was just me left. What became apparent is that I'm not my bones, my hair, my muscles, my organs or my cells; I'm something unexplainable - I am me.

I'm sensitive - so sensitive - I have courage, I'm brave, I am loving, selfish, I'm driven I'm ambitious. I am...

Today I am following my soul's calling to heal, to coach, to give back what I have been given by others and to inspire.

I could tell many stories, but I would like to share two. One is of an international footballer, aged 25, the other is about a 5-year-old girl - my daughter.

One story is about growing up and developing. The other is about being beaten, shoved, doubted and laughed at because of who he is.

I see so many similarities between them; they're both uniquely strong and fiercely independent. They're both kind, generous, warm and caring. Emotionally, they're both very intelligent.

One has lost himself, the other is on the first steps of the ladder in second guessing herself. From day one, my goal has been that she can stay as closely aligned with her true self as is possible in this ever-changing world.

Wanting to grow and develop, I think my daughter is on the right track. But, now the tests come; she's now in a system; the education system. In year one, academically, she's a dream pupil. Some, of course, have naturally high IQ levels but everybody can ultimately improve at this. At her year two parents evening I was told she is 'Academically speaking, a year in advance of where she should be.'

That's nice, I thought. But, it's of minimal importance to me in comparison to her self-assurance, her confidence, empathy and kindness.

Then the bombshell hit; 'She's very assured. She thinks she knows everything at times and can be bossy to others and tell them she's better.'

I sighed a deep sigh. What I heard the teacher say was: 'She's strong, she's not easily told what to do, she's happy to let others know she's the best.'

But, the reality dawned on me as I was sitting in that chair. She's in the system guided by others. If my experience is anything to go by, she could potentially have her dreams beaten down. Having great confidence and then being told not to have it can make people scared to trust people of power. It can also dull the confidence in children - and in adults, for that matter.

I could feel my role as a Dad was just about to be tested.

On the other side of the spectrum, a friend of mine. He is 6ft 4, 15 stone, quick, strong, aggressive, a good passer of the ball, intelligent, reads the game. He *has* everything.

Eight years in professional football and he has been shoved from pillar to post.

He is strong-willed; incredibly so. His will is a gift. He soared to the top of his game in professional football, but ultimately, he needed a leader who saw his power within and didn't feel threatened. Often, he was told 'How dare you just do whatever you want to do.' For me, and for him, that translates to 'How dare you be you.'

Year by year, he has tried to run from the pain he felt inside of being different to the others, and from being alone. He pined for a boss who would walk with him into the unknown and manage and guide his soul.

As years passed, he has turned his back on his soul and instincts. He neglected who he was. The fear of being rejected and left out to dry was so severe and so sharp that his escapism was to completely abandon and numb his senses.

Mental health and addiction, for me, walk hand in hand.

Earlier I talked about Churchill; my overriding sense of this quick, brilliant man is loneliness. Yes, his ego drove him for years, but his true self led him in the end; he sucked it up and let go of the burden of being himself.

I was sat with this particular client after a series of events which led to the manager at the club he was at edging him out. He was having issues in his personal life.

His life, in general, was leading him to believe he was bad and it was his fault. Thoughts like 'I'm a troublemaker, I'm wrong...' would fill his brain.

I said to him, 'who is 'I am?" I know him as well as anybody and I wanted to know who he thought he was.

I told him I thought he was ambitious, courageous, brave, sensitive, empathetic, caring and that he had all of the makings of a true leader.

The 'I am' statements are the classic egotistic statements.

'Watch how many 'I am' statements you make in one day.' I said, wondering how many were self-depreciating rather than kind.

He soon realised that he has been painted as a bad guy because he didn't accept being talked down to and he was aggressive.

I said; 'It's tough to be you, mate. Really tough. You will have to learn to accept yourself and follow your paths. But, never accept anything other than the truth led by your gut instinct. The voice that says 'run faster' 'win' 'humiliate the competition', why do you deem that has a bad voice?'

Many people get caught up in people judging them, but ultimately, who is the judge? What if that attitude creates an absolute winner and a leader who will never accept ordinary?

These attributes are gifts, but they made him - and they make many others - different.

The only voice that you should be wary of can come at any point in life, but may come when you really succeed. It's a voice that says: 'You are so much better than everybody else. Are you sure you need to contribute as much as the others?'

That voice is the silent killer for many people. That voice was the silent killer for me.

That subtle foe can cause you to become complacent. Here's some thoughts it might give you to watch out for:
- You've earned the right to…
- You're the main man
- She loves you
- They love you
- It's his fault
- He's rubbish
- They aren't as good as me

To lose that ease and to let the mind made sense of who you are (ego) takeover is the downfall of many people. For me, so many of my mental health issues come when I identify with my ego.

I say to people I work with all the time, I say it to my daughter after she breezes a test or a dance class; well done - you practiced, you worked really hard and you were you.

My daughter came home from theatre school on Saturday with a sticker saying 'Number One Poppet' (she's in Poppet class).

'Wow,' I said, 'what was that for?'

'For being myself.' She responded.

The school she attends for two hours per week, comes with great praise. It's led by an ex-actress whose desire it is to create esteem and confidence in children as she never had it.

Of all the lessons, the lesson I know I'll have to teach my daughter is humility; our place in the universe. She has talent and strengths - as we all do. As she grows, it will separate her from her peers in certain areas.

My biggest fear is that unconscious teasing that might lead her to second guess herself. By teaching her the quality of modesty, I hope she's able to continue on her path, truly aligned with herself.

In summary on the two subjects mentioned; my daughter and my friend, there's a resonating truth. They both have individual, powerful souls; they're captains of their own vessels.

The self-identified, strong personalities are the ones who change things in this world. They have the courage to disrupt as they speak their truths. They can influence self-belief, leaders, fear, and ego; they're all so delicately linked.

Self-awareness and emotional intelligence are things in the corporate world and society in general that are becoming more prevalent. People are far more aware, but we can always do more.

The split from self to who, history has shown, has the greatest of impacts in dictators like Hitler. I understand this is an extreme case, but it really highlights this subject.

However, as a parent and a coach of young people with dreams it's tragic. To quote my favorite actor, Al Pacino in his Oscar winning performance in the film The Scent Of a Woman:

'There is nothing like the sight of an amputated spirit. There's no prosthetic for that.'

Once your journey of losing sight of yourself begins, the journey to find yourself begins, and it's a journey your soul cannot lose. So, it becomes a need...

Chapter 8- The Illusion of Needing to get somewhere

There's no where to get. No where to reach. Visions aren't goals. Dreams and visions are the universe showing us what will happen if we do two things. Trust ourselves and work tirelessly.

To need...
"To require something because it's essential or very important rather than just desirable."
A necessity...
"The basic human <u>need</u> for food."
At which point does it turn from a desire, a calling, a passion, a gift, into a need?

To need is an obsession. How can it not be? It's described in the Oxford dictionary extract above as essential. If something is essential, we will do WHATEVER it takes to get there. It's like when an animal needs to eat to survive, it will do whatever it takes. The scavengers - like vultures and hyenas - show this.

I turned out the light and rolled over to my side. As the curtains gently rippled, the Alpine summer wind gently blew through into the room

I felt lonely. My body ached after today's process of growth and development. On June 12th I was 8 days into a 24 day training camp. It was all part of the search and the need. I had to satisfy.

I said earlier in the book, in the self-belief chapter, that these chapters are all so closely linked and entangled. Belief, to ego, to need.

It wasn't an official training camp. I wasn't paid to be there as part of pre-season. In fact, I had paid to be there; money I didn't really have. I paid for the accommodation, the flights, my food for a month. It wasn't cheap. Why?

I had seven weeks off at the end of the season. I *needed* to get better and come back stronger, fitter, I needed to hurt myself physically and mentally so I couldn't be broken. I needed to taste pain and smile at it.

Or, so I thought...

After three weeks of partying and drinking, I flew to Zermatt, Switzerland with my friend and personal trainer at the time, George.

One day I was 2900m above sea level at the foot of the Matterhorn mountain. I'd just had my third session of the day and it was 6pm. I'd done three sets of 10 200m runs. 30 runs at altitude is extremely tough.

'No one will break me.' I said to myself, 'no one will touch me. You can't break me.' My internal dialogue was rampant and positive.

I packed up my rucksack and had a swig of my drink. I started to make my way back to the cable car to make my descent back into Zermatt town.

There was an elderly man taking a break from a hike. 'Impressive stuff.' He said in his broken European accent.

'Tough.' I replied.

'I'm sure! What are you training for?'

'I play football.'

'Oh.'

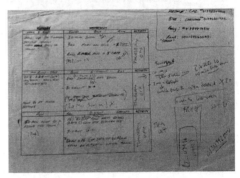

Me at the foot of the Matterhorn where I was running 200 metre sets. I was obsessive with my daily plans and training notes .

Then, the line that I will never forget, that made me reassess and soul search for weeks; 'Does Steven Gerrard do this?'

Time froze. My legs went to jelly. 'Erm, erm...' I paused.

He looked at me, genuinely inquisitive into the life of a footballer.

'I'm not sure. I would think so.' I eventually replied.

My soul laughed at me, it saw straight through my lies.

'Who do you play for?' He asked.

BANG, another punch slammed into my ribcage. I knew he was waiting for Liverpool, Chelsea, Milan...

'Southend United.'

'Oh, cool,' he said. 'Good luck with it all.' And off he walked.

I stumbled, dazed. My mind was rampant like a cackling hyena. I could hear the laughter around my head.

'Who do you think you are? Who are you kidding? Southend United?' It was laughing at me. 'You've spent for weeks up here whilst Steven Gerrard, who is 10 times the player you are, is laying on a beach.'

The shaming voice, the ying to my yang, the shadow to my light.

I sit here today, 13 years on from that experience and I can put myself right there on that mountain. My belief system was shattered by such innocent comments.

What was I doing up there? Sure, to train and get fit but it's a bit extreme. I did it every summer for seven years. Every season that followed was the same; inconsistent; highs and lows.

Insanity is doing the same thing over and over and expecting different results. What would I do today? I'd still train; I'd train hard. But, I wouldn't isolate myself in order to 'find' a place in me that others couldn't go to.

The place was already there. Steven Gerrard had his 'place', he didn't need to find it. He, I'm sure, was riddled with self-doubt and anxiety from time to time.

That search and that *need* on that mountain was me, searching for myself.

You can have all the physical fitness in the world , you can eat as clean a diet as is humanly possible, your sleep patterns can be measured and aligned with the most productive and efficient way. However if you lose belief, if fear beats faith and you have to use your body, athletically, all the physical conditioning and preparation in the world will be totally worthless.

These bouts of physical paralysis happened to me on many many days. We see it today a lot also. How many times do the judges watching players perform say 'he was off it' 'maybe he wasn't fully fit' or 'he was rubbish' 'he's out of form' more recently England legend Wayne Rooney has gone to play in the United States. Commentators and journalists are commenting that he looks "rejuvenated" "reborn"

Having watched clips myself he looks quicker and sharper and leaner than he did in England. I can relate well.

When I left Lincoln City and was at the end of my career I didn't return for the "de briefing" what was the point? I wasn't coming back.

The assistant at the time, Paul Brush, Called me. In his "assessment "of me and "things to work on" I never forget. He said 'you looked leggy and heavy, you couldn't jump. I suggest you work on skipping and jumping this summer, quicken your feet up and maybe leave all the heavy weights you do alone"

I wasn't surprised by his assessment. Such is the ignorance still today.

I replied 'Paul, I was gone, I am gone, emotionally broken, I couldn't possibly jump or run I was running and jumping with a million voices on my shoulders. When you have such doubt and fear it's the most debilitating thing there is to energy. It has NOTHING to do with weights or skipping. Surely you get that'?

'Well no, you looked heavy and you weren't fit' his voice was raised and I could hear a man out of his depth. It just left me feeling crazy and alone again.

I don't blame Paul. Again it's just ignorance around this most important of issues. A former player at West Ham, Paul is today a senior coach and leader in Tottenhams academy.

In 2004 I joined Chester City in league 2. Managed by former England international defender Mark Wright. We had a strong squad.

I was bought with a simple remit 'you're a big nasty bastard, exactly what we need. Last season you bullied teams and scored goals'

That summary of my skill set I often got. It always left me a little confused. I wasn't nasty and not a bastard. I was driven and ambitious. People were always shocked when they met me away from the pitch. I lost count of the times I would be told 'what a nice guy' I was and 'I looked a lot bigger on the pitch' I'm 6ft 3 so I'm not sure how big I appeared. Although when someone believes in who they are deeply on the inside it's amazing what it can make them appear like in physical stature. That's aura. Aura for me is someone who knows who they are. It's said in a magical way about a handful of individuals, which reinforces how scarce true belief, not ego actually is.

So I went to Chester. With all my demons In toe.

Within twelve weeks I'm at rock bottom. Out of the team. Shattered all the time and so so sad inside.

I had put so much pressure on myself 'that this season would be the one now' that i was debilitated, completely overwhelmed.

I couldn't last an hour without being substituted through exhaustion yet I was training twice a day and very very fit if tested.

The usual tactics were employed. Shaming. Shouting. Ignoring. Passive aggressiveness. All are emotional abuse so my shame just grew. The shame? That I was a freak.

One day it was decided to "fitness test" me.

I had gone out on the Sunday drinking. A rare rare escape from the prison of my mind. Nothing like numbing the brain and its relentless stream of thoughts.

So Monday morning I was still, probably a little drunk.

We did the fitness test and I smashed it. You see I didn't care. Alcohol can do that. Take us away from reality. I had switched off thinking. Switched off fear.

I was me.

It's why there's so many alcoholics. It shuts off truth. Gives us a false insight into "freedom"

I never forget the manager and his staff looking at me like I was crazy. Scratching their heads, thinking "how is this possible"?!

The spirit is the captain of our vessels. Without it at peace we have NO chance of fulfilment.

A desire, a passion, a nagging voice inside that all is not well is another thing. A pure thing; a creative thing. Only through 17 years of constant failure, when on the outside, everything looked so, so good, has taught me this. I've had to pull myself up out of the dirt of failure so many times sometimes I don't quite know how I came back.

Desire; it's who I am.

You see, I had desire, passion and competitiveness in abundance - in huge abundance. In this case, the blessing is also the curse. It's so, so hard to control that monster that rages inside and the passion that burns.

It's my belief that a real competitiveness - a God given gift - of desire and ambition, can so quickly turn desperate. It can turn into a need and an impossibly essential thirst.

There is a reason there are teachers, managers and leaders in life.

But, they are all labels - it's just a name. The action behind the title is critical. Each of these titles carry great responsibility. How can we teach others until we've been really taught?

To teach...
"Impact knowledge to or instruct somebody how to do something."
"Cause somebody to learn or understand something by example or experience."

The last point in an interesting one; impart knowledge by example of experience. I would say, what experience? Has that manager, leader or teacher looked at the families, gone on a great search to discover why they never fulfil their dreams and why they never had the confidence? Or, figured out why they could never find consistency?

This is not a blame game. I'm merely sharing my truths. There are so many confusing messages and teachings about.

Teachings like how you must <u>have to </u>want it. How whatever you want must consume you and how you must obsess in order to make it.

These are some of the teachings I learned via coaches and media when I was pursuing my dreams.

At about 10 years of age I remember sitting in my bedroom and thinking I needed to make it as a footballer. From 6, I lived, ate, slept and breathed football. Stereotypically I had the kit and the shiny boots; I always had a football with me.

It was my passion, after all. Coupled with that God given competitiveness and my ethically good attitude, I was also tall, had great endurance and good hand, eye co-ordination. It was a good situation for a young man with dreams.

My passion, my calling, my gift, my love, was turning into a mind-made ego-driven, fear-based necessity. I always practiced fiercely, driven by a pure love and a passion.

Passion...
"A strong and barely controllable emotion."

My passion was strong and barely controllable when it was pure. Then I felt alone, unloved; I think I felt subconsciously unloved; I felt as though my needs were never met.

Love and passion *love* to need. I think we haemorrhage talent because some essential needs are being unmet. I see it day in and out. Passion scares the life out of this who have 'found 'themselves in managing files or got ALL the qualifications apart from the most essential one- understanding themselves. Understanding their shadow side , their darkness. For me, 'big personalities' are easy to manage. If you ask them how they are feeling. What their fears are and how you can't help them but, we have systems ran by individuals who are not emotionally developed enough nor wise enough to know what shame is , it's catastrophic affect. Leaders, true leaders not a label, will challenge and confront so you must use the key ingredient to manage them and I use manage loosely. Build an emotional bond. However, you can ONLY do this once you're intimate with yourself. Once you know yourself. How the hell can you get to know another when you don't know yourself. My experience of being an outlier was one of being shunned and treated ALL the time with passive aggression , the most cowardly form of emotional abuse. Lied to and smiled to yet stabbed. This is going on day in and out as more 'box tickers' find themselves in positions above their emotional 'qualifications'

As a performance coach (not a psychologist) today, I attempt to lead clients back to a place where it was effortless and where it was driven by love. I teach them to clear the doubts, the fears and unconscious teachings.

There is such a subtle and fine line between want, desire, a calling and a need. Media feeds this confusion. We are given messages of the great artists, performers, actors, business leaders and visionaries who were obsessed. We're told how it was their relentless need to get there that got them to where they are.

I would like to use a few examples; Steve Jobs, co-founder of Apple, Richard Branson, founder of Virgin, myself, and a young client who is 20 years of age with a natural desire and competitiveness.

Steve Jobs co-found possibly the most life-changing brand in a long, long time - Apple.

He was given up for adoption, which might've naturally cued young feelings of not being enough and not being worth loving.

"What's it like when your mother puts you in someone else's arms and walks away?" Steve Jobs was quoted saying. This fear, this eternal trauma of loss and pain is the road to loss of self.

I get the feeling, based on my own journey, that a great confusion started then for him. When he came across a teacher who really 'saw' him and believed in him, he was quoted saying: "I just wanted to learn and to please her."

That's a classic example of love to need. What I hear in that sentence is; "I have a massive calling and intend to learn and to push."

Jobs was saved by Apple. At 30, he had unarguable abilities but had also suffered abandonment.

I don't need to dig much further into Steve Jobs. I guess, what I'm highlighting is that I don't subscribe to the standard thought process that it was these rejections that 'made him'. I say it was in him anyway. He had a gift, a calling, a vision and a passion - he was just lost.

In his commencement speech in 2005 at Stamford University he said he never graduated college. What I hear here is that he had a calling that a system couldn't give him.

Chapter 9- Creativity, God, Naturalness and Talent

Creativity can't exist where there is thinking and direction.
Creativity is who we are. Creativity lies in instincts and feelings .
Fear destroys creativity. Like fire destroys ice.

'The point of life is not to get anywhere, it's to notice that you already are and always have been. You are always and forever in the moment of pure creation. The point of life is therefore to create who and what you are, and then experience that.'

I toyed, many times, on whether to tackle the subject of 'God' in this book. It would be dishonest of my journey not to.

Until 33 years of age, I had no faith or trust in anything, other than the mind made me. If I work harder, do more, push more, outfight and sacrifice, then I can 'get there'. I talked at the start of the book about the moment of achieving that occurred for me. I 'woke up'. What did I wake up from? The best part of 33 years of darkness.

I became enlightened. The light was switched on in the darkness. What was the darkness? For me, it was the complete dominance over my human mind. The relentless internal chatter of 1000 monkeys daily. 'You'll never get there', 'She doesn't love you', 'He doesn't like you', 'You're a loser', 'He's better looking', 'They're better friends'.

My ego - that mind made image of what I was - had 100% taken over. And, after having all of the external things removed, I came back into a light. It will be ok. It will all be well, even though you think it won't, it will.

It's time to be kind, be honest, work hard and help others.

Imagine for a second I had gone into any of the matches I had participated in and had that voice running the show. It's not a complete absence of fear but a serenity and peace that were the main driving forces.

The times I found myself was in the absence of thinking. That for me is God.

A place of instinct, creativity, peace. Our true selves.

It can't exist with Ego (thinking) Remember Ego Being the mind made false sense of who we are.

It's why I explain to my daughter when we cuddle, that that feeling she has, I have is God. I'm aware the teachings she will come across at school.

How does it FEEL baby? 'Warm, nice daddy'

Warm and nice, no thinking FEELING.

The best players, the best in all endeavours whether aware or not are without thought.

The prayer that the best do, is to silence the Brain and to wake up the soul. The creativity, the effortless performance.

The last seven years since that moment, I feel like I'm walking into my true path, where I'm at my best creatively. In biblical terms; 'God's will not mine be done.'

I've explored the faiths and my new journey. I've come to a place of neutrality around it and I'm comfortable with my views.

I want to reflect upon Usain Bolt, Lionel Messi, Steve Jobs and Mother Theresa; there would have been many other examples. I've chosen an incredible athlete, a footballer, an innovative leader in business and technology and a modern day saint and humanitarian in Mother Theresa.

These people are an array of gifted humans. A gift is given and received. Who's it given by? I don't believe there's a man in the clouds with a white beard handing out special talents. I do, however, believe that all of us have a creativity and an ability to do the most wonderful things. Sing, dance, run, be kind, be empathetic, play football, create technology, have great computer skills, be a fantastic Mother; the list goes on and it really is endless.

The common theme with the images of Messi , Bolt and Mother Theresa hands clasped in prayer or pointing to the sky, is that they're all 'thanking', 'giving gratitude to' and 'handing over their success to' a power greater than them.

This transcends organised religion. Gifted, insightful beings have walked amongst us since time began. They've walked in various human forms; woman, man, child, able-bodied, disabled.

It's not a coincidence for me that the four people I've chosen to look at are all 'humbled'. They can all say that they turned up and they worked, and worked, and worked.

The great misunderstanding, for me, lies in the belief that you should just sit back and let things happen. I've fallen down this trap many times; from the extremes of trying too hard to just thinking it will happen and so not trying at all.

Creativity lives in a neutral place. Activities like prayer and meditative silence can create a direct line to the source of creativity and peace within us all.

Steven Gerrard was recently interviewed on what's missing with young players nowadays. He says that it's because they don't obsess about it.

'I used to obsess over football.' He said.

I'm a huge admirer of the man; both as an ex-professional with an understanding of what a tough career it is and also of his creative gifts.

I would suggest, that sure, he trained and was motivated, but what was left after all of that was him; the soul, the body. 'It' was in him. What is 'it'? For me, it's what is in all of us; that creative core which is unexplainable.

'How did you score that goal, Steven?' 'How did you execute that pass?' 'How, when 3-0 down in that European final did you find it inside of yourself to lead the team back with an amazing display?' 'Why when others around you were flagging did you have a place to go to , so deep, so profound, so crazy that you could pull it out and change history,?

David Beckham, after his one man display vs. Greece to claw England back and into the World Cup with that incredible free kick.

'How did you do it, David?'

Practice, of course. But... and then what?

There is a sense in both of these examples of the divine and the spiritual. Their ability is above the realms of understanding. It's an instinctive drive of energy and purpose greater than ego, glory, fame or money.

In different circumstances, in my story in the chapter on self-belief, that 95 minutes full of a million thoughts, sitting on that toilet seat, door locked, searching inside my very being, I was praying for answers.

They were given; water was turned into wine. Of course, not literally but a poor performance turned into a great one. I had tapped into my very being.

'Be still and know that I am God.'

'I am, who I am.'

These are two extremely well recited extracts from the bible.

There are many incredible sources of wisdom. These writings and scriptures are some examples. I take what feels so true to me and these seem to have made a profound difference to my clients today; these clients are people with great gifts, trying to make sense of it all.

The two statements I've picked are so profound to me.

'Be still, know that I am God.' For me, this translates to my journey and also the journey my clients are on.

Your head, your brain, your mind that constant chatter is not where you live. Buying into those messages, beliefs and thought is not where your best performances lie.

Be part of the team, talk to others. Don't isolate yourself in your thoughts. Work hard - work really hard - and when the voice says 'I'm tired' beat it. Say no. Say be quiet and just keep working. Trust that all will be well.

So what I've done is talk the truth as I believe it to be and talk in the absence of fear. In the absence of fear, we can be free to be truly ourselves and create what we are truly capable of.

As a doctor, a nurse, a mother, a carer, a singer; whatever your destiny, you are capable of achieving your goals.

By focusing on work and being part of team, we switch off the mind - or certainly quieten it.

'Dear Universe , you are my heart, you are the voice inside that knows what's wrong or if something feels right. You are that feeling I get when I give or receive a cuddle. I pray you can show me my heart. I pray I can work hard always but never turn away from my heart and what I love to do.'

Those three letters, G O D, are so scary. They were to me. I think it's because of what the concept means; what it means to others and the media describe it as.

God, to me, means the best version of me. That effortless place where I'm free to create. Where fear can't penetrate, where there's no outcome. It's where what we want, at the deepest level, will be given.

I believe anybody can apply this as a concept. Whether you're a parent, a leader, or you'd like to apply this to your own life. Start by remembering a time if your life when what you were doing felt effortless; either in your career, your hobby, in relationships or in friendships. Remember how it feels to be told you're loved. Remember how it feels to feel you *have* to do something.

I am brutal in my demands of my clients today. In terms of the hard work, I'm pretty unforgiving. I tell them that the rut will come, it will happen - in life, it's unavoidable. But, focusing on beating the voice that wants to pull you into your fears, is key.

In footballer's terms, when the voices start say 'NO! Not today. I'm just going to work, run, keep focused. If I give into you, I will fail in being me.'

In the workplace, thoughts like 'What's the point? I will never get that promotion.' And 'My client will never buy that idea.' Can plague your abilities.

Chapter 10- Winning

I am not bound to win, but I am bound to be true. I am not bound to succeed, but I am bound to live up to the light I have.

—Abraham Lincoln

And Then What...?

As I bear my guts and soul onto these pages, I'm not trying to intellectualise anything. This is merely all I have to help others. If that is what it does or doesn't do, my experiences, my losses, my victories and my growth is all I can offer.

As I sit and write this, I'm listening to Foy Vance, a beautifully real and grounded artist. He says 'I decided when I went on this tour to just come to the stage with myself, no pre-thoughts or ideas, just turn up and see what comes.'

He's winning. In fact, I would say he has won. Why? Because he understands that the point of life is to not get anywhere.

Just turn up and create; let it flow like a river cutting through a valley. Thinking would lead to taking the edge off of the natural process.

What if after 70 years of 'turning up and seeing what happens' he touched millions of souls? Every day, he wakes up aligned with his gifts. I must add, though, people who are aligned with their gifts are not immune to being human, to loss, pain, grief, sorrow and all of the things that make us vulnerable and the species we are.

I wrote this book with the title of 'And Then what…' mostly because of this chapter here; winning. So, what's my truth?

My truth is that when I did what Foy is doing; just turning up and seeing what happened without needing to get somewhere, nine times out of 10 I was a very creative human being. I have the gifts to lead and the courage to walk with bravery. But, trusting that it was that easy was another thing altogether.

'Winning' looks different to all of us. I know that we aren't all born with ultra-competitive spirits. This book, however, is my experiences and maybe if you're reading this you can identify with it.

We were in the woods a few Sundays ago. My daughter (5) and I were with my good friend, his son (6) and his niece (6), his parents and his sister. It was a lovely dry, crisp November morning.

My friend's Father kept pointing out houses made of sticks previous 'explorers' had made. As the kids ran off, he sent his son to the 'house' further on with three coins.

'The lads love that.' He said.

I asked what he was doing.

'Oh, we hide the coins in the tree houses and then they find them and can keep them but they think they've been left by the Gruffalo!'

Brilliant.

The kids loved this and by the end they each had about a pound's worth of silver coins. We were nearing the end of the walk and there was one last tree house ahead. The kids ran off.

The two girls ran back excitedly. My friend's son remained over in the trees. 'Come on…' my friend shouted and his son slowly walked back to join the group.

'I've got six coins.' My daughter shouted.

'I've got six too!' The other little girl said.

The little boy - let's call him Jack - said, 'I haven't got any. They fell out of my pocket.'

'Oh no - let's go and look for them.' I said.

My friend had been walking a bit further ahead with the other adults.

'Mate,' I shouted, 'Jack's lost his coins.'

He walked back towards us and went to his son. He explained later to me that they hadn't 'fallen accidentally out of his pocket'.

'I know him,' he said to me, 'the girls beat him and found the coins first so he threw his away because they beat him.'

This five-year-old boy was so disgusted that he lost he had to make it clear that he wanted nothing then. It was either all or nothing.

Society says these are the leaders, the winners, the high achievers. They're also the addicts and the drop outs.

His Dad is the same way and he spent the first 25 years of his life tortured by this uncontrollable desire and passion. This competitiveness.

His father was in our national football team within three years of his 16th birthday. He wasn't a child prodigy, in fact, he was overlooked in the system. His desire was misunderstood, by himself more than anybody else.

His son, however, has a chance. All it takes is a bit of awareness. I, on the other hand, had no chance…

I needed a guide who knew what it was to carry this juggernaut of competitiveness around inside careering into every other car on the road.

My mother tells me of when the school football coach pulled me to one side. I was seven. Whenever I missed a good chance to score a goal,

I was so outraged, so disgusted. I would drop to my knees and punch the floor repeatedly. It was considered 'unstable behavior'. What a shame. What it actually was, was the captain of my ship, my soul and my destiny screaming 'No, no, no, you are better than that.'

I needed somebody to take me to the side and say, 'What's the problem?'

'I can't accept missing that.' I would have said. 'I just don't accept it.'

'So let's start practicing and sharpening your skills…' My imaginary coach would have said. 'Then, if you miss them it won't be through lack of effort and you can handle that.'

'Great. So, I will get home, do my homework and then from 7pm - 7am I can practice?'

'No!' My imaginary coach would say, 'you just need to do a few hours daily, weekly, monthly, yearly. Don't worry, don't overwork. Just do enough.'

I needed somebody to say, 'even if you do miss, you need to accept that life will do what life does. you can't control winning or scoring, perform the best you can and then let go.'
Winning; to be victorious. Victorious over who? Over what?

Years of chasing this illusion that winning in a team sport would make me fulfilled. It never did. Some would say that makes me selfish - shouldn't I be thinking about being part of a winning team rather than what makes me fulfilled personally? I agree, I should.

But, my measuring tool was merely that truth deep down. That knowledge that my performance today was *all me* and it was easy, effortless and natural in its execution, but ironically filled with physical effort.

To me, that was winning. It was a personal standard, not a taught one. My issue was that I never knew how to win. I never knew who to walk that path of least resistance the majority of the time.

I never knew how to win, even though deep down I knew I had all of the tools it took to be a real winner. What even are these tools?

A relentless lack of acceptance of who I was? To search and search and search? It was the search for 30 years that led me to this point. In the last seven years working with individuals and teams and giving the team what I so desperately needed at the time.

There wasn't a university course that could have given me the answers; there was no theory or professor. Brutal experience, pain and soul searching plus a necessity to survive are what led me here.

I think the reason 'winning' is so difficult is because with all the talents and gifts we possess, we also walk a road laden with potholes and landmines. It doesn't come easy, winning is not easy. Becoming the best version of ourselves isn't easy.

In fact, it's a lot easier to abandon ship and to run. My God, the amount of times I wanted - and tried - to run. The pain. Fear; fuck everything and run.

Fear of failure, fear of humiliation, fear of abandonment, fear of ridicule. Fear of how hard it will be, or how hard it is. Fear or standing out, fear of not standing out. Financial fear… the list is endless.

For me, the struggle was that I knew on the deepest level - so, so deep - how good I could become, but I didn't have a coach who was led by the powerful, spiritual truth.

I look at Usain Bolt's coach, Mr Glen Mills. In the film about Usain, it's clear he is a man with great wisdom. He has a calm, assured nature, a spiritual sense of all being well. The scientists can't measure it, the coaching boards can't certify it, it just is. He is at peace. That's peace, in my opinion, will calm and lift everybody in his presence.

Bolt praised Mills, saying it was his coaching that make him improve, not just as an athlete, but as a person.

Momentarily, I found the ability to win zapped with a cattle prod. When I was at peace with myself and calm, it would all start to happen.

I had 22 employers in 17 years. When I found myself, I would win. I would then lose myself and drop away. The next employer - who would have seen me winning and being the best version of myself - would then 'rescue' me and put me in his team. Buoyed by getting another chance I would soar… only to fall again.

Here's a note to my 20-year-old self:

"Relax, it's all there. Let's seek a great physical coach and get you in great shape. Daily, you will have your good technique by the nature of the fact you are a paid professional. Let's keep your body in great shape. Then be you; don't chase it. Don't panic. Focus daily on running and walking, chase the ball. Pray. Have silence. Don't judge those who haven't got what you have or those who aren't capable of pushing as hard. Don't begrudge those who have more. You are on you own path and you will get there. Don't let your evil mind track you into isolation. Thinking that if you hang around with people whose standard don't match yours, you will automatically become like them. It's impossible; you are you. Be with them, fight with them, be part of them.

Your mind will want to pull at you constantly, tricking you into thinking you have to do more and that the reason these guys are at the top is because they do more. It's lying to you. They're there because they don't try to become more than who they are. They are just themselves and they work hard.

What if you were just yourself and you worked hard? The drive is in you. Be at peace. Understand that it won't be easy and that you'll suffer with anger and fear. That anger and fear will make the boat rock, but it won't flip over.

Work hard and don't compete with anyone else, despite what your head tells you. When you sit there in the dressing room before going out on the pitch, make one promise that you will fight the voices that want to pull you into the past or future for the next 90 minutes."

It was March time, eleven games left. We were five points adrift at the bottom of league two. It was a crisp morning, spring was in the air and the training pitch had the signs that it was nearing crunch time.

At this point, I was in one of my purple patches, a run of form that I knew I was capable of; the time when everybody would sit up and take notice. Of course, it would soon drift away. That was the pattern of insanity in my life. On this day, however, the tank was still a quarter full. With five goals in my last seven games, the media had started to label me a talisman.

We'd have three back-to-back 1-0 victories with me scoring all of the goals. Looking back now, I understand; I was aligned with the warrior that I was - *I am.*

The evening before, It had been announced that we'd signed a top young player from a Premier League side on loan. He was a creative player, somebody who would give us more opportunities to score goals.

Training commenced at 10.30 that morning.

I always started my pre-training routine at 9am.

Breakfast 9 - 9.30am,

Gym 9.30 - 10.15,

Pitch 10.15 - 10.30,

Start 10.30.

I'd found that this discipline really worked for me at the time. I walked onto the pitch - it had been a good week with win the Saturday before when I scored and played well.

The warm-up began; a light jog and then some speed drills amongst directional work. I believed in the mentality that everything you do you must be at your absolute maximum. I was always able to do this - apart from the days I was depressed and vacant.

I was 26 at this point and my career was so up and down, so inconsistent. It was 10 years by now. So many nearly moments when I thought I had cracked it. I'd find my best level only to be overwhelmed by the voice inside.

After a 20 minute warm-up we're now to do some 10 by 10 yard boxes; a common drill in football. In this drill, five players try to keep the ball whilst one player sprints to get it back. It's tough, fun and it sharpens the mind, body and touch.

This new player was in the box I was in. It was his turn to get the ball back. He jogged about, laughing, with his boots half undone. It was all good fun.

Now, I must pause. Yes, it was fun, and football is so much fun. It was a laugh and a joke and it was great to get out there and kick the ball around. But, here's what I believe. I know as I work with so many young players today, they don't know what seriousness and hard work looks like.

The assistant manager blew the whistle and said 'Ok boys, have a drink, relax.'

And Then What...?

I was raging, focused, tuning in for tomorrow's big match; we needed every point as we scrapped for our futures and our lives. League two is the bottom of the four professional leagues in the UK. If we got demoted down at the end of the season then it's an abyss - we'd be entering the realms of semi-professional football. No longer can you say you're a professional.

A lot was at stake. I was a powerful character and said to him, 'Hey, come on, mate. We've got a big game tomorrow - the work starts now.'

He laughed at me. Then, if I remember correctly, he threw a ball at me or in my direction.

'You ok?' I said.

'Calm down, mate.' He replied.

'Calm down? There are jobs on the line here, and livelihoods.' I walked towards him, he was still laughing and mocking.

A red mist descended and I head-butted him. It all happened so quickly. He went down, there was blood and shouts from everybody. 'Woah... wow, what the hell are you doing, Drewe?'

'Fuck this.' I said and I walked in.

'Get in, *GO*.' The manager shouted as I walked. My head was already spinning.

I pressed the button on the shower and the hot jet covered me. I stood there, hands against the wall, and let the water soak away every part of me. I wanted to wash away what just happened, as well; wash away this beast within. It was the only one I couldn't control fully. It had led me through match winning performances where manager after manager, some ex-players who were internationals and knew what it took, said I could be whatever I wanted.

It also followed me to deep depression and anxiety when my performances were so bad and when I walked about in a daze, confused and consumed by a thousand voices.

I was kicked out of the team to an inevitability of weeks and weeks of soul searching. But, I will always come again, I always will, it's who I am.

I sat in the canteen and started to eat my lunch, the voices were *really* talking. What's going to happen now? How are the lads going to be? What will the manager say? Will I play tomorrow? Within seconds, the room was a blur.

All I remember was one minute, putting a fork in my mouth with some food on. The next minute, I was off my chair and on the floor. What felt like water was covering my face. It was blood. I saw out of the corner of my eye the player from earlier sprinting off down the corridor.

Three hours later and less than 24 hours before a big match, I left the accident and emergency at the local hospital with the physio. I had eight stitches on my eye. My eye was closed. Apparently he'd run in and hit me with his ring that he put over his knuckle.

I played the next day, we won the game if I remember correctly. The player in question didn't play and was sent back to his parent club, his employer.

I was pulled in front of the board and the fiery CEO - who had a background in HR - on the Monday morning. I explained to them that this is high-performance and jobs are on the line. I said that one bad apple in the group would drag us down. The supporters work hard all week to pay our wages and it's a lack of respect of them. It was a disgrace.

Of course, I took matters into my own hands and that was wrong. My reaction was wholly unacceptable and I apologize with all of my heart to that player involved.

I've not mentioned all the names of clubs or players in this book where I felt it was inappropriate, it's not what the book is about- not at all. It's not wholly a football book or a biography. I didn't have the kind of career that anybody really cares about. This book is to merely highlight my journey. The lessons learned and what I see now with so many people.

The topic is titled 'winning'. I used this story because I've had experience of winning. Winning is a relentless effort to give all you have, striving towards your soul's knowledge of the events that are always going to unfold in front of it. Then, you have to get up, go to sleep and press repeat.

I say to the guys today; it never gets easier but it never gets harder. It just *is.* It is what it looks like. I've been blessed with this beast inside that is in pain whenever I take a shortcut or cheat, whenever I have cake or biscuits or miss exercise, can't solve an injury assessment or a psychological issue with a player, I will beat myself up.

And Then What...?

I often wonder; does it hurt others the same? I'm sure it doesn't. I had an exact conversation last night with a client; a top, top player who's currently going through a rough year or two. He hasn't ever been able to manage himself and his beast within. I feel he's starting to now. Maybe, potentially, we'll start to see.

I attended my daughter's school sports' day the other day and was surprised to see no races. There were no winners or losers, rather a set of challenges for all the children to have a go at. A few days later I was sat with my daughter and I said, 'I thought you would have had races at sports day, honey. I know you love winning.'

'Me too, Daddy.'

'Why do you like winning, hun?' I said, excited to hear her response.

'It makes me feel nice. I want to be the best runner.'

Not prompted, not cajoled, nothing suggested - 'I' she said, her true self, wants to be the best. Not better than herself, the *best.* It's a powerful statement and it's one that I can relate to on so many levels.

Now, she has two parents meeting all of her emotional needs. She knows she's loved unconditionally, everything's provided. So, there's no searching for love; she's not shamed toxically and told that she's not good enough unless she wins. She hasn't slipped into perfectionism. Her soul just craves that feeling and how winning makes you feel.

I have the same thing. I understand you can't guarantee winning, you can only give your very best. She's yet to fully grasp that concept despite all of the subtle teachings I've given. What comes, however, with that desire to win is an absolute disgust of losing. Perfectionism, in a natural form, looms large. Perfectionism in the seeking of self and the loss of self isn't what I'm talking about here. But, it's this constant craving to fulfil your soul's preemptive destination.

Many times I was on the winning team, and many of my team mates were overjoyed, even if they personally didn't play to their fullest potential. I was never happy with that. *Never.*

I could be on a losing team, but if I had been somewhere near my best, I would have been internally satisfied, despite the result. I can't control everybody else, only me.

There's a great curse with the gift of winning, though. It's my huge belief that mental illness and those gifted with a huge desire walk hand in hand.

Chapter 11 - Trust, the most precious of things

A controller doesn't trust his/her ability to live through the pain and chaos of life. There is no life without pain just as there is no art without submitting to chaos

-Rita Mae Brown

Why is it the most important thing in the world? Because without it, we are prey to fear, insecurities, anxiety and a life unfulfilled. We 'lose' trust like we lose car keys. Where does it go? How do we get it back? Why is it so important? Why is it so hard to keep?

I've said at many stages of writing this book that all of these topics are so intertwined. Self-belief and trust, winning and mission or position. All of these topics are really my journey through where I fell short and was misled by myself and others.

'I'm going to give you some advice...' is such a well-used statement. Lawyers press the timer before they start 'advising' and you'll pay a hefty price for what they will offer up.

'I advised him and he didn't listen and now look...' or, worse still, 'I'm telling you, he's too quick, too strong, don't try to take him on.' In football terms, these offerings would be served up regularly.

Is it a coincidence that the best athletes are called 'aloof' or 'arrogant'? It's no coincidence for me. What I see is somebody who has complete trust in themselves. Somebody who knows what they are and what they're not. These people have heard a million 'experts' and listened to loads of 'advice', but they never stray from their instinctive nature.

When I think of my best days and my best games, they are laced with irony around this whole subject. I would sit in the dressing room with a peace in my heart, my mind like the ocean with gentle, lapping waves. Not the 25ft tidal waves I spent most of my career fighting off!

Sitting reflecting recently back in a dressing room. It prompted me to think of the mindset pre performance.

'There a two big centre halves. Don't fight them, Drewe. Kick it to the wingers from goal kicks. There's no point in putting balls in the air, they will win them all. Ok Drewe?'

'Yes, of course boss.'

Inside I'd say 'I'm going to destroy those two centre halves. I'm going to make those mother fuckers wish they hadn't got out of bed this morning , they won't compete. I'm going to tell the goal keeper to ignore that and kick to me.'

I smile as I watch my soul answer back. The madness in my head - the complete lack of responsibility - is that what it is?

No, not for me. On those rare occasions I trusted myself I knew that I could take them apart - I wasn't about to buy into the fear of others. That's their shit.

It's really lonely - trusting yourself. When you have belief, true belief, unpopulated by others' unconscious projections upon you. You see, I've learnt all of this stuff by failing constantly, managing to stay on my feet for a brief moment in time.

Picture a cinema screen. Its vastness, its blankness; waiting for the projector to illuminate it. A child is similar. They're vast and blank, just waiting for a belief system. The tragedy is that so many times the belief system that is projected onto them is generational. It's repeated generation after generation.

A child's first view of a higher power and great wisdom is their parents. Parents often 'advise' from their 'experiences'. When I look at myself in the past, I couldn't see my part in huge experiences. My fault, my control, my fear, my lack of trust. The denial was my cloak protecting me from those bitter, cold winds of truth.

To advise...
'To give counsel, give guidance, guide opinions, tips and to give direction.'
'Her Grandmother advised her about marriage.'

If her Grandmother has looked completely at her part in the good and bad. If she has been guided by an unusual force, her instinct and her heart. If she 'advises' from a place of humility and if she suggests places she failed and just shares that, then the Grandmother is one of the lovely ones.

'Take what you like and leave the rest.' This is one of the best suggestions I've ever heard. What a humble piece of advice. In short, the person is saying; 'Here's my experience of what you're telling me about. Here's what I did and what I didn't do. Here's why I did this and why I didn't do this. Here's what was driving me. I'll share my strength and hope with you. Take what you like and leave the rest.'

This book isn't to advise anyone of anything. You might get some identification from my feelings and my thoughts and it might validate yours, help you find courage, now that would be wonderful.

I remember walking into recovery from emotional damage. At the time, this damage was critical and threatening my life in so many areas.

I had been told over and over and over again that I must be wrong and that I must give up my way of doing it. 'Ha, that's easy for you to say,' I thought.

All of my life I had been programmed - computer style. Specific inputs brought forth predictable responses. My mind still tends to react as a computer reacts, but I'm learning to destroy the old tapes and literally reprogram myself; leading me back towards trusting myself.

I enjoy being led and guided by a universal power, an instinct. Today I choose trust.

Trust is divine, it's holy. It lives outside the realms of human understanding and science. And, so it should.

My daughter by the age of 4 loved the monkey bars. I supported and held her as she went across. One hand under her bottom one on her back. At the start, it was slow but fun, it was 95% me and 5% her. As the weeks grew it was 50/50 and then by 6 weeks it was all her. Now, she has been at gymnastics since 3 so her strength was very good. Her bravery, I just like her Dad's at that age is fearless. I asked my father recently what I was like as a child and he said two things which really resonated. 'Brave, fearless, completely fearless. Oh and sensitive very sensitive.' What a cocktail!

This process lasted for about 6 weeks then she was kicking me off. One Saturday afternoon, we had had lunch and I said, 'come on hunny, let's head to the park'. We entered the fenced off play area and she was gone. She headed straight for the monkey bars. She climbed up the ladder to the start platform. I speeded up my walk and was there by the time she was ready.

'Daddy leave me, I do it.' She protested.

Cool. Awesome. Her spirit is kicking in just like her Daddy, I thought.

'Ok hunny, focus and stay strong'

'It's a long way, Daddy.'

'Yeah, but if you fall it's not far and what's the worst that can happen? It might hurt but that's ok!'

'Ok Daddy.'

In the moment, my four-year-old daughter hands me her trust. It's a big task, but it's achievable. It's a 2 metre drop onto soft wood chips. I do envisage her falling and it stinging, but I want her to trust in the face of fear.

I'm aware I can have the 'fear nothing' attitude, but I'm comfortable; even though the looks of others might disapprove.

She got half way and then boom, she slips and hits the deck. It was about 4/5ft drop into wood chips. She laid there a little winded.

'Daddy...'

'You're ok honey, there's no blood. You're just winded. Get up and go again.'

I walked over, lifted her up, kissed her on her forehead and said 'go on baby'. She climbed up the ladder, steadied herself on the platform, reached with her right hand, her body dropped down and her left hand joined the right, she was on her way again.

BOOM. She got half way, and again, fell.

By now some gathering mothers saw her wobbling and ran to help.

'Leave her, she can do it.' I said to them. They stopped five yards away.

They shook their heads and tutted. I walked past them. I smiled and they awkwardly looked at their feet. I had no time to deal with their fears. I felt that feeling I feel a lot these days and did as a player. I felt different and alone.

'Honey, as you grow you will fall, you will hurt, and you will fail. Life will create pain. Smile at pain. Wait for pain, attack pain. If you want to do anything in this life it's going to hurt.'

I picked her up, cuddling into her, I said, 'baby I'm so proud of you, I love seeing you work hard and fall and feel pain and get up and try again. Come on my princess let's go and get ice cream.'

Fast forward to prayer time five hours later. I kneel next to her bedside. My hands together tightly in traditional prayer fashion. Her little hands mirroring mine as she lays, secure and warm tucked up in her bed. Safe.

'Dear God (higher power, something, space, the universe, a cuddle, love, a greater good - call it what you want). Thank you for the courage to trust my heart and to follow it. I know I will fall but I know I can do it if I practice. God, keep me close to your heart. Don't let others tell me I can't. Don't let others make me question myself just because they question themselves. God, we pray for them. Thank you for my life. Universe we pray that all those without a roof over their head tonight, who are cold, alone and scared, can find hope. In the dead of night. We pray for all those who are sick and won't get better. We pray for the children who don't have the security we have. Thank you so much for our lives. Keep us safe and give us the courage to follow our hearts. Amen'

I kiss my daughter on the forehead and say, 'Out of everyone you ever meet in your life, know that I will never leave you and will always love you.'

She smiles and scrunches up her little shoulders without knowing that it's a reflex to her soul feeling so loved and secure. It's these feelings which are the perfect conditions to maintain trust in a world that will do its best to pull her away from it as the unconscious projections begin.

'I think you're a wonderful character, Drewe. When you trust yourself, work hard, chase and trust your teammates you're a really, really good player. Don't worry if you give the ball away today. I did it a million times. Just pick yourself up and get the next one. I will never criticize a mistake, never. I made many that could be criticized. However, what I won't accept is you not puffing out your chest, pulling your shoulders back and saying 'give me the ball'. I see you, every day, in before anybody else and leaving later. You eat right, you train hard. It would be a tragedy if you didn't fulfil that potential of yours by not trusting yourself. If you run and run and don't go under I will not let you down.'

I sit here imagining coach after coach I had saying that to me. I say it to the clients I work with today. Because I see their character, their hearts. They deserve all the love and my trust.

I shared that imaginary one on one with any of my past bosses with six players today; a 16-year-old, a 34-year-old, a 20-year-old, a 22-year-old, a 29-year-old and a 32-year-old. They are all professional footballers.

'What I would give to hear that.' I said.

'But why, why can't any of them say it?' One client asked, 32-years-old, 10 years in the English Premier League. A sensitive guy, a human being, who just needs appreciating and trusting for being - not doing and achieving.

'It's so simple, isn't it?' He said.

'I think so.' I replied.

'They just need to appreciate the players. Give them some love. Because that place inside them is dead, mate. They're afraid to speak such words, to appear vulnerable, to share feelings. Mostly because they don't know what they feel anymore. The feelings become deadened like nerve endings.'

'It takes a big man - and a leader - to be so in touch.'

Chapter 12- The Pressure of Pursuing Dreams

The greatest pressure is that of the knowledge of your potential. It's both a gift and a curse. Don't bury it for it will destroy you . Own it. Accept it. It's a beautiful gift. But, you must understand NOW you can do nothing other than truly give your best. Beat that voice daily that wants it to be easier. Push yourself so that voice can't dominate you.

-Drewe Broughton

'It's funny, mate. Two or three players I grew up with were all so sure of themselves - I was always so envious. Now, they're using people to help them with the mental side. Why do you think they're doing that now?'

I've been working for three years with this particular player. He was 19 when we began. Now, aged 22, he has surprised many of the tipped and expected players he grew up with. When we met, he was struggling with deep anxiety. He was suppressing energy that was presenting physical symptoms; the classic psychosomatic pain. A young star, driven and led by a deep calling; a love, a passion and a dream.

'Pressure is a privilege.'

If I could tell you how many times I have read that quote or somebody would send it to me. It always triggered some feelings; anger, distaste and disgust that these people with no idea of the torment it takes to survive could send such a quote.

Is it a privilege to be wracked with fear? To have to bury so many fears deep down? To have to put on a front?

'You ok big man?'

'Yeah, good thanks.' Would be my stock answer.

'How are you?' Man, I hate that question. Do I ever truly say who I am?

'Really struggling actually. I feel weak and pointless and I just want to curl up and hide.'

I remember saying something quite similar to my manager after a lunchtime performance. He was horrified.

'You can't think like that.' He said, his face in complete astonishment.

See, here lies the problem for me. So many leaders and coaches just haven't faced their fears. They don't think about them daily, weekly, some haven't even considered them for 5 years, 15 years, 30 years. What's needed in this scenario - and in order from them to help others - is a complete written inventory of their pain. It's a long process, sure, but once it's done and their fears are really dealt with they will be better equip to help themselves and others.

When a person doesn't face their fears, it often affects the person or people working under him or her. A key example of this is the young man I mentioned earlier in the chapter.

I can see what people meant now, as a 37-year-old. Pressure is a privilege because it means you're blessed with a gift, with a calling and with a dream.

That pressure will never leave you until you fulfil your destiny and until you maximise your gifts.

I still have that pressure today. But, I know how to deal with it now. Daily, I sit down and write out my fears. I look at my anxiety and know it's a physical result of dishonesty, resentment or fear. I always get led back to the same place. All day I'm watching for where I fearful, dishonest , selfish(the wrong kind) or self seeking. I correct myself on the spot. I'm only human but I'm blessed I've been led to this code for living, for remaining loyal to myself. After all I'm the only one at my birth and I will be the only one at my death.

Ultimately, it all comes back to the same thing I've been saying throughout this book. It's important to keep going, work and work, don't quit and know where you're going.

Yesterday, I sat with a 20-year-old client. He's a top, top talent. The day prior, he had been described to be by a well-respected manager as 'the best player I've ever seen aged 15'.

I've worked with him for two years. At 17, he was starting to fade away. He was confused, scared and in a daze. Lacklustre training session after lacklustre training session and people were starting to judge. Not guide; just *judge.*

He has been very good so far this season. It's not the midway point and people are talking about him but they're not raving. They should be raving, with his talent.

Pursuing your dreams isn't for the faint hearted. You must continue to face your truths, nobody else's. Your soul's discontentment, your pressures.

I said to him that he is going to be under huge pressure until he stops playing. The pressure is his spirit pushing, nagging and niggling him. The headaches and the stomach pains that so many people get when they're feeling this pressure in a withdrawal into yourself.

I didn't tell him that it was a privilege, but that he has the capabilities to change people's lives in many ways. His soul knows that.

On Saturday night he said he had ignored his partner all night. She hadn't seen him for a while and I'm sure she was looking forward to it. But his soul was screaming at him. It was applying so much pressure.

'From 14-16 they tried to take it out of me.'

'Who?' I said.

'The staff at the academy.'

'Pass it, pass it. Loads of boring passing drills. I just wanted to run with it, flick it past people and have fun. Programming my brain to do a certain function that wasn't what I would do. It's not who I am. Eden Hazard was brilliant at the weekend. He was everywhere, expressing himself, giving the ball away and getting it back.'

'I know, mate.' I said.

'This pressure you have, this fear that you will never fulfil what you know on your deepest level you are able to be will eat you up. But, here's one way of staring it in the face and fulfilling your destiny. But... it brings great pressure.' I said. 'You will need to step into your light. To shine. To do it your way. To nod your head at all the instructions and still do it your way. To take the praise and the criticism that will come. Even when you fail and you give the ball away you've still got to keep doing it your way. It's time to look into your head and say "I will not let you down, I will just be me".'

'I will do it my way.' He replied.

'It's a lot of pressure...' I reminded him.

'But I don't care about the crowd, or the players, or the manager. It's me. It's killing me every week I come off. It pains me to know I'm capable of more. I've been doing extra in the gym, extra practice, extra everything...'

I nodded, 'I know.'

'It's all positive. The challenge I have is to stand up and say "fuck this".'

It takes courage - so much courage - to be you. We live in a world of fear; conditioned fear. The poor people who live like this don't even know what it is. They buy more stuff, they eat more, they train more, take more photos for social media, talk more, laugh more, pretend more. It makes them sick; physically, spiritually and mentally.

It's all fear; fuck everything and run.

You have to face your fear otherwise you're never going to fulfil who you are meant to be.

Try SPAF instead; stay put and fight.

The people with presence are the ones with gifts and who know how to fulfil them. They walk tall, with a aura. That aura is the courage it takes to win their battle and to be themselves. They've had to fight hard, really hard, against the fear.

Let's go back to the opening paragraphs of this chapter.

'Why are these players suddenly now looking for help?'

Because they were surviving on ego. They were surviving and running on image, not truth. The truth will haunt them and the fear grows as they play in bigger games with more attention on them. More expectations. Eventually, this pressure gets too much and they struggle to cope. Their ego-built fuel is running out and they need to say *I am afraid,* to somebody - anybody - who will listen.

I would love it if coaches and leaders would stand in front of players and validate fear. It's the validation that will lead to freedom.

Saying 'I'm afraid that if we go out of this competition, I'm done. My managerial career will be over. The press will spit me out, I will be a joke. I'm afraid. However guys, I love you lot, working with you, seeing you fail and try and scrap, I would back you guys every time. I'm in with you let's go and fight'!

It's this kind of vulnerability and culture I'm introducing into big corporations. From directors to senior management. The truth? I'm not sure how many want to have a belief system of a fragile ego ripped apart in order of truly fulfilling potential. It takes huge , huge courage to go on this journey.

Chapter 13- The 'Edge' and staying on it

'The beast in me is caged by fragile bars. Restless in me by day and by night. Rants and rages at the stars. God help...........the beast in me'

Johnny Cash

In terms of talent identification in sport, there's a simple remit worldwide; 'find the players with it.' So many of the more creative souls in the history of the world spend their lives trying to figure out how to stay on it.

An edge is sharp. It can cut; cutting hurts. Physically it can hurt - to be cut open and to ooze blood. Emotionally, though, it can hurt, too. People with an edge can cut people with their ruthlessness and their internal drive. They can cut people simply by being who they are, by their passion and their calling.

'Don't get sent off, big man.'

'Don't get involved...' Number two shouts.

Boom ...insecurity and self-doubt get an anchor now starts confusion. How could I not get involved?

Was there something I could do to make sure I didn't get in trouble?

When I was in a strong place, I would smile and say nothing. I would know that I was going to compete with everything I am and that I would 'walk the line'. In this strong place, I'd also challenge the ball with everything I have. Sure, that'll make people wince and cause issues but I will manage those issues. In short, I will walk on the edge.

One night I have my 'edge' cleverly taken away. The team were playing away from home, I arrived at the stadium two hours early. I was walking from the coach to the dressing room. At the time, this particular club was managed by a manager who had previously managed me.

As I walked past his office, the door was wide open and he was sat with his assistant.

'Big man, lovely to see you! Come in and say hello...'

I was four months from the end of my contract. I was scared and under pressure to play well. At the time, I was scrapping for my life. I'd played the week previously and had been somewhere near my best.

'How's it going?' He asked.

I nodded and said I was fine.

'Look,' he continued, 'I was at the game last week and I sat and said - shit, he's still got it. Look, the owner is here tonight, the TV cameras. Frankly, our young defender won't cope with you. Take it easy on him, yeah?'

I was sensing something.

'When's your contract up?' He didn't break for breath. I knew what was coming next.

'In the summer.' I said.

The summer was only 6 weeks away. He smelt my desperation, the fear and desperation all players have around being out of contract. The insecurity runs rife in the lower leagues.

'Well, if you look after me tonight and don't beat up our defence, then there will be a contract for you here in the summer. Closer to home, isn't it?'

'I can't do that.' I protested. 'You know this business. Anyway,' I began to back out of the room, 'all the best.'

As I walked away, the voices in my mind were rampant; 'It hasn't been a great season for you.' 'You have bills to pay.' 'It's a good offer.'

My edge was becoming blunted.

I was substituted that night on 60 minutes. I didn't play with the edge that I had inside me. I was judged by the edge and just couldn't find it.

The fear of throwing away that contract offer cost me. I knew that I was at an age that made that a good offer and it played on my fear.

I couldn't beat it. Fear took away my edge.

That manager won that day. He manipulated me, he emotionally abused me. He played on my moral compass, he played on my desperation and fear. He won that battle. He beat me.

To be honest he crushed me. Monday came and I was excited to call him and discuss our 'deal'. There was a nagging fear. It was that feeling when you just know. I just felt on a deep level that I had been manipulated and lied to. This manager had cheated. He had, in effect, offered me a 'deal'; don't play well and I will give you a contract.

Yet my contract clearly states 'I promise to give my very best to carry out my duties as a professional footballer' or something very close to this. He had played on my fear. He had gone into my soul and pictured me at my age then with a wife and bills and he had promised me security. He had emotionally abused me and violated my trust.

Imagine, for a second, I'm a 5 year old and he promises me if I help him clear up all this mess in the house he will give me some sweets and then he disappears. How would that 5 year old feel? Sad. Used. Cheated. Abused. Worst of all their trust in life would disappear. The greatest tragedy is to steal trust from another.

Through no trust in his abilities or who he was, he stole mine. He lied and manipulated and conned to win. Is that success? Maybe he would have moments of success financially in his career. But this man's emotional success is at minus 50. You cannot really 'win' without a strong moral compass.

The "old school" brigade in our society who moan about millennials might say, ' he tried to get an advantage and that's good play' ' you should have ignored him and battered them' ' but you are too nice and was weak there' I would say.. ' oh really, too nice have you read this book, the head-buts , the aggression, the pushing of Myself to bear insanity. I am human and I am moral and I believe in the right way and fairness. It's why I refused to cheat and fell out with managers over it'

That old school way was built on blocking out emotions and feelings and becoming an emotionless assassin or be broken. No middle ground. Ask Vinny Jones, the notorious hardman who has sat in recovery meetings for addictions... what's the route of ALL addictions? The death of self and an inability or unawareness of feelings and not dealing with them.

The illusions of winning financially are mythical. I've had money, girls, cars and crap. True winning is led by a realignment with our moral compass. That Monday afternoon consisted of an enthusiastic voicemail followed for good measure with a text message. By 8pm, nothing. So I sent another text.

The truth was creating anxiety in my heart. By Thursday, 72 hours had ticked by along with three more missed calls and two texts. I surrendered. I was devastated. Karma. Those girls I told I would call after manipulating them into sleeping with me. Those times I had lied and manipulated to feed the desperate addict within. The noose was tightening around the neck of my career. Of the false identity built on pillars of sand.

I felt like an ant. Running around, digging holes, small and fragile, I felt that everybody's life was bigger and better than mine. If success means money, girls, fame, drinking and nightclubs. Then, who am I?

My edge is me; a supreme winner. I'm so competitive. So, so, so competitive. I have an almost psychotic calling and drive.

I would get my head cracked on the pitch and my first thought would be 'this is awesome. Can I taste my blood?' I would taste it. The more I was battered physically, the more my soul enjoyed it.

I'm a warrior. I'm ferocious when my soul is aligned with the path that is greater than I know. If I feel injustice or wrongdoing, I will fight like a dog. If written off, I will come back like nothing you've ever seen.

I know this about myself, and yet managing this volatile edge and 'walking the line' is a different thing entirely.

November 2003 is a month I'll never forget. I had received my second red card in four games for stamping on Gareth McCauley, who was then at Lincoln City.

Gareth; I'm sorry. What an incredible career you've had. I sat and watched you have an outstanding Euros, envious that you were never insecure like me.

The next day was tough. We lost the game. I was called in by the manager and told I could leave and that I'd never play for the club again. He said my behavior was disgraceful and that I had issues.

The next two to three days were awful, like many other days in my career. I was soul searching, desperate to understand *why* I did that. Why did a voice in my head say, as we landed from an aerial duel, 'Prick? Fuck him.'

Why, why, why?

I was shunned. I was made to train with the 17-year-old trainee players in a separate area of the training ground.

Over the next week I went through all of the voices, the demons. I endured all of the lows. Towards the end of the week I remember saying 'No. No, no, no. Fuck you.'

Ron, my advisor and friend, called me.

'Mate, so and so wants to sign you. And, so does so and so.'

'Great,' I said. 'Tell them no.'

'Sorry?' Ron questioned.

'Tell them no. No one tells me who I am and when I'm done. No one.'

'But Drewe, you won't play for this club again. These are good offers.'

'Nah, no chance. You think I'm just going to leave? I'm staying. They're going to need me.'

This sentence was followed by a long sigh from Ron, 'it's your call.'

God bless you, Ron. Even though you aren't here anymore, I'm sorry for putting you through it.

The voice started up again again, that voice deep down. It was telling me it was fight time. I started a six-week programme.

I trained twice a day with the youth team and then spent time at the gym. I lifted weights, I ate right. All the while, there was a voice inside screaming; 'they won't take me down. I'm not that guy.'

The club signed three guys in my position during this time. Still, I kept training, driven by my soul's craving.

On December 17th at 9am the phone rang. It was a Saturday morning. At this point, I had weekends off.

It was the manager.

'Hello.'

'Drewe, it's the boss.'

'Morning, how are you?'

'Well. Chris and John are struggling with slight injuries and can't play today. David has just called and has been up all night with a sickness bug. Get to the stadium at 10.30am. You're playing today.'

I will forever remember that game. I was fitter than I have ever been. I had earned the right for my soul to be at ease. I had trained, sacrificed, slept, trained, sacrificed, and slept for six weeks.

I played 90 minutes.

We won; it was our first win in 5 games and I was brilliant. I scored and I was a warrior all game.

I forgot to mention, during my period of six weeks out, I had to report for home matches. After another bland performance, when the team lost, the injured players and players not involved would have to be in the changing room after the game. One match, I was blamed for the loss.

'I have to say it, I have to say it.' The assistant manager pointed at me. I was standing in the corner of the dressing room with a suit on whilst 18 players sat slumped, having just walked off of the pitch.

'You. It's you. You drag the mood down. You cost us'

At the time I was shocked, 'WHAT? I've not been training with you for four weeks. I've been nowhere near any of it and yet it's my fault? Pathetic.'

'You can't talk to him like that.' The manager intervened.

'It is pathetic.' I said and I walked out.

So, to come back on that day, absolutely *not* wanted and in dire circumstances forced me to deliver. And when I did, it felt amazing.

So after that great game, that amazing comeback that night the team flew to Dublin, for the traditional Christmas party. It was great to be back. Back with the group. Back in that most amazing of places, where you know you've just been at your very best. The captain, after a few Guinness's thought it would be a great idea to call the First team coach , the guy who had just weeks before , singled me out in the dressing room for blame when I wasn't involved in the match!

So he called him and I believe the conversation went something like, "John it's the skipper, look its Drewe'

'Drewe'? The coach replied

'Yeah he's gone missing. He just slammed down his Guinness and said you know what I can't take it anymore, I've been thinking about the way he attacked me in the dressing room a few weeks ago. It's scandalous. I'm not having it. He then just walked out. That was 6 hours ago'

Of course I was in on it and we dragged it out for 48hrs more. When we came back into training after a few days off, we still maintained no one had seen me! I then jumped out to surprise him. The poor guy hadn't slept for days!

A good lesson for him!!

Six goals in the next eight games. I'd gone from outcast to talisman.

The tragedy is that football scouts up and down the country were taking notice. The eyes were on me as my run continued, I was now 14 games into this streak. Then, the voice started…

'Who are you kidding?' It asked, one day.

That voice has sabotaged my life so many times. What is that voice? Who is it? Where does it even come from?

It's from the lack of true belief. It arrives and it leads me further and further away from the source of all belief. Trust is a spiritual sense and I had none.

My perfect state was when my back was against the wall. I loved it. I tried to create it many times just so I could 'find' myself. That was when the ease would come out.

Recruitment departments in all industries need to find people with edge; the game changers. From the trading floors to the creative fashion houses, from the record labels to the football clubs.

Eminem has the edge. Cantona has it; I grew up idolising him. Roy Keane does, so does Paul Ince - I saw it when he managed me. Mandela does, Richard Branson does. It goes on. I just see leaders.

It's very difficult to manage these types of people unless the manager has been there and understood.

I look at rugby, at Danny Cipriani. Sir Clive Woodward (the World Cup winning Head Coach in 2003) said he saw him when he was eight and couldn't help but say 'wow, what a talent.' Conflict, fines, addictions and inconsistency has followed him. I believe it could have been prevented if those managing him had the edge and had learned how to walk in similar shoes to him.

'Tiger Woods has it.' They said, when he was playing in tournaments aged eight, surrounded my older boys.

What? What is it that he has?

'To be honest,' he said, 'I just wanted to *destroy* the field.'

Destroy is an aggressive word. I would think Adolf Hitler had a similar vision to destroy the world and civilisation and morality as we know it.

So technically, if you use words like 'destroy' you are going to be very, very misunderstood by most. How, as we grow up, do we deal with such an aggressive inner voice? Personally, I felt ashamed. I was made to feel bad about this desire. I was different and so I *must* be wrong.

But, who are the judges and jury on what is right or wrong? They're just mere mortals, like me and you. And guess what? These mortals have unresolved issues and ignorance.

It has only been my complete destruction of my humanly formed ego and an extremely painful journey back to myself that has led me to really understand (not completely, but a good amount) myself. I have to pray and meditate regularly. I have to silence society and listen to my source.

That voice can sabotage and has proven that it can sabotage in the past.

When I hear sabotage my brain jumps straight to falling off the edge. Sabotage is to 'deliberately destroy or wreck'.

That word - deliberately. Deliberately to 'consciously and intentionally'.

Consciously - 'in a way that is direct, perceptible to and under the control of the person concerned.

And there we have it. Those with the 'edge', those who sabotage themselves when things are going well. If you really trust the process and study the words, you can end up back where you started; in control.

In recovery from addictions, which for me was a physical escapism from an emotional and spiritual bankruptcy, we start... with stop.

By admitting that you're powerless over sex, money, alcohol, winning, controlling, smoking, gambling, smoking, eating etc., you can discover your life has become unmanageable.

The second step in this journey is to believe in a power greater than yourself than could restore you back to sanity.

Was I insane? Yes. If insanity is doing the same thing and expecting different results, I was - without a doubt - insane.

Had I lost all power to be consistent and not escape? Yes.

As I desperately sought to find myself, to stop sabotaging and to be consistent, I tried to control more and more and more.

I was chasing my tail, digging myself into holes to deep to navigate and calling them wells. If only I could have known that my spirit was bankrupt, broke. Then maybe I would have stopped running.

I heard Alastair Campbell, the now-journalist who rose to fame as Tony Blair's spin doctor, talking on a podcast recently. He said he sabotaged his own life. This realisation led him to talk about solutions, and he still sounded a little lost. Why did he sabotage? Why couldn't he continue to walk that incredibly fine line and stay close to the edge, where generally speaking, the amazing things happen.

In my experience - and perhaps this is the same for him - it's because I hadn't accepted myself. I hadn't accepted the voices in my soul, the ones that truly knew what I was capable of. Instead, I wanted to rush.

All you need to do is breathe. Live in this day. Slow it all down. Stop the dis-ease from happening and be you. Let others call it 'the edge'.

Chapter 14- Vulnerability Is Where True Success Lies

Anyone, who tries to take control of what cannot be controlled, brings trouble to himself. Today let us engage with life and merely do our best, with a peaceful knowing that that Is all we have.
This leads to freedom from the prison of our minds and back to our true limitless creative, instinctive selves
I will accept both the embrace and the insecurity of not being in charge

Vulnerability comes from the Latin word wound.

Vulnerability is a state of being open to injury; physically, mentally and spiritually. If we're not open to injury then we're closed to it. Anything closed is shutting the door, turning your back of your truth.

All of my 17 year playing career I believed I needed to be stronger, work harder, be faster, eat better; control, control, control. The thought of losing or never achieving my potential was unbearable. I just couldn't show weakness. I trained in a t-shirt in minus temperatures, I could never say I was tired if I was. I was dishonest, really, and that was all born through fear of somebody seeing the true me; my vulnerability.

Today I live in a place of truth. I give thanks daily for my health and in prayer I just ask for the courage to know my heart and follow it. Today I am vulnerable. It's funny; when I'm asked to meet a new client with their family or representatives, I always smile at how long it takes to remove their protective layers of ego and get into their truth, their heart and their vulnerability. When you press that button there's a squirming.

I know which players can get to the top. It's the ones who can look at their biggest fears and not run from their true selves. There are those who get there without it, but there will be an escapism in their lives which cost them in some way.

The twelve step recovery programme used in the Anonymous Fellowships for recovery from a spiritual and emotional bankruptcy - addiction - is the most powerful system I've seen. Its core is vulnerability. Without admitting to yours you just won't recover. You'll stay on the rollercoaster. It's about the death of your false self you've held up to the world and finding your true self. It's accountability at its most brutal, but most effective if - and only if - you're ready to be vulnerable.

'Hi, my name's Drewe - I'm grateful to be here.'

'Hi Drewe.' Says the crowd - the thirteen other people in the room.

'I'm struggling today. I'm scared, I want to run and hide and just not come back. I can't control these voices laughing and saying "Who are you?" "You're not a good leader, you're a joker." "Who gives a shit what you have to say?" "Your clients will all leave you and you'll be where you deserve to be." But, I know now, seven years after coming into this fellowship that this is where I need to be. I'm safe to be me. I can speak the unspeakable.

I can be vulnerable and accepted as a perfectly imperfect human being. Thanks for listening everyone.'

Silence.

'Hi, I'm Julie ...'

Take a deep breath. Five seconds in and seven seconds out. It's lifting, all of the fear. Man, no wonder for 17 years I was a manic depressant, bordering bi-polar. I was a near lunatic at times. All of this stuff locked up inside.

The next 40 minutes ticks by. I just close my eyes and listen. With every share, I grow in identification. A lovely blanket of serenity and peace engulfs the flames of fear and doubt that are burning me alive from the inside out.

It's 9pm on a rainy Tuesday evening in October. As I get in my car and leave North London, I'm at peace. As lovely as my day is, I have a series of meetings but in a one-to-one format, face-to-face or on the phone, I expose my soul - all of it - my clients do the same and it lifts.

I work with some of the toughest spirits I've seen. They're tough, tough beings but they're human and vulnerable. It's that vulnerability I tap into. The undeniable. I'll leave the scientists doing their thing. I wasn't chosen for that journey. I want to tap into the spirit. I abandoned mine many years ago because I had no solutions for my nakedness and my vulnerability. Flesh cuts, bones break, muscles tear, vessels bleed, loss hurts, grief debilitates, we die.

We are, by the sheer nature of being human beings, extremely vulnerable. We can build our bodies physically to show the appearance of power and invincibility but one disease, one cancer, one bullet, one hurricane, one drunk driver, and we can be wiped away.

We can grow our brains with knowledge and we can hide behind our title or PhD, but we still can be wiped away from the world easily. We are vulnerable. So, so, so vulnerable. We're nothing really, just a spirit locked in a bag of bones and some muscles with the controls to gather data until old age, disease, famine, hunger, accident or war kills us.

I learnt through much pain and much searching about vulnerability. It was terrifying. Everything I had to protect me was taken away. Physically, the roof over my head, the money, the career. I was so vulnerable. I was given shelter, physically, by my friends and family; a sofa to lie on, a roof over my head, but I was still naked, exposed. I had to be me. Everyone is searching for magic answers in the world of high-performance. Answers they think live in a world of science. I feel for them.

It's in the gap that man has tried to bridge for years - to rationalise - that quest alone leaves man vulnerable because we just don't know. There's great comfort and acceptance to be found in our powerlessness, our weakness. There's a tremendous power that overwhelms when we remove our pathetic little man made egos.

Seven years prior to this meeting I had a one-to-one meeting with my manager at the time. After a poor performance on the Saturday he asked to see me on the Sunday morning.

'What was that, Drewe?'

'It was poor, boss, I know.' I said.

'Why? What the hell is going on? You didn't win a header, you couldn't run, you couldn't keep the ball. If you don't set us off, we don't play well. You're the trigger player for us.'

'Yeah, I know, but I woke up Saturday morning and I was flat. I laid in bed until 11.30am and I just didn't want to get out. You know those days when you have nothing?'

'What?' He said.

'Those days, boss, when life just flattens you and you don't know why. You just try to get yourself going but you can't.'

'You can't think like that. Who thinks like that?' He said.

I felt shame immediately; what a bad person I must be. How weak, how pathetic, how different.

'We've got a big game in five days, get yourself out and put a big week in.'

'Ok boss.'

Sitting there thinking it's not ok to be afraid, feel weak, less than, not "up" for it

I walked out and felt an overwhelming sense of loneliness. I was so confused, it was toxic shame. Healthy shame is good and it's important as we develop as humans that we learn what wrong behaviour is and what is socially acceptable.

An example is my daughter. 'Honey, make sure you shut the door when you go to the toilet.' I often say these days.

Now, she might initially feel that she's wrong and perhaps she'll feel a little embarrassed, but the key here is the action and behaviour are bad or wrong. But, *she* is not wrong, she is not bad as a human, she's not a terrible person.

When I left the office I felt wrong. I felt bad, my spirit was wrong to have those thoughts and feel that way. I was a bad person, I wasn't like others. I felt toxically shamed.

John Bradshaw, I believe one of the greatest thought leaders and therapists of the last century, stresses his point in much of his work. In his book *Homecoming* he speaks about toxic shame and how it destroys the self. It destroys creativity and individuality. It destroys souls and makes a person start to think that they are flawed and defective as a human being.

The real issue for me always comes back to a lack of awareness from leaders, educators and teachers. Again, in the field of professional football - an industry I've been in my whole life - I see players toxically shamed constantly. I reiterate again this isn't a witch hunt of a blame game. I have empathy for the unawareness of the coaches and the leaders, but I hope and pray that the education can be altered and a whole personal therapy chapter and area can be added in the education. Otherwise, for me, this epidemic will continue, just as insanity does.

The people who make decisions seek comfort, they seek to narrow the odds of failure. I understand why, having lived in that world my whole life and having to face the metaphorical guillotine week in week out, like a gladiator in the arena. Thumbs up or thumbs down; it's a horribly simple living. I needed to guarantee success so I turned to science. I saw a nutritionist, a sports scientist, a physiologist and a psychologist - I employed them all privately. All of these people had studied. They had PhDs, they were expensive.

If I could make my body, mind and brain as strong as possible, my energy system - through food - so efficient, I thought then I would win. I would narrow the chances of this embarrassing loss and humiliation. If I sprinkled my talent on top, surely I could nearly guarantee it. The final bit of this puzzle is to take it out into the stadium and put it on show.

Poor old me. If only it was that simple.

Today, I will surrender to my feelings, even the painful ones. Instead of looking to escape or act them out. I'll be vulnerable with another. I'll share my feelings, I'll call a friend - a safe friend. I must do this safely, with those who have the capacity to relate, identify, understand and also have the courage in their lives to do the same.

In my vulnerability and my truth lies a powerful solution. I will pull away the cloak of falseness and walk tall as a human being. I won't kid myself.

It was in 2012 when I started to rebuild myself from the ashes and the belief system of invincibility. I wanted to rebuild myself as the child I came into the world as, a child built on vulnerability.

'Good morning guys. Drewe - how are you feeling this morning?'

'Erm, I'm ok thanks James. A bit tired, but ok.'

'Ok isn't a feeling, Drewe. And tired is a physical reaction to lack of rest. How are you feeling?'

Silence.

'I'm scared. I feel really frightened. I'm scared of where I've got to in my life and what lies ahead.'

'I understand. Thank you, Drewe. John, how are you feeling this morning?'

It was 7am and three men between the ages of 23 and 28 say on three sofa in the cottage at Sporting Chance Clinic. James, the head therapist who is still there today, addressed the group. It was day one of 30. It was time to learn vulnerability, to learn fragility.

I'd escaped it for all of my life and ran and turned my back on the truth. I could lose. I might not get to where I know I can. I might finish my career underachieving. I might not stay married. I may never have money. All this was complete uncertainty.

As the weeks unfolded and this became a daily discipline - sharing feelings in groups, in writing, with strangers and one-to-one therapy, a sense of peace transcended me. All of a sudden I just knew all I had was me and my daily disciplines to keep in a fit physical, spiritual and mental shape; the three parts of the human being that need care. The fear of failure, the future, winning and all that stuff that consumed me to the point of insanity left me a day at a time. I say a day at a time because you never earn the right, as I'd always wanted.

I had this idea that if I worked really hard at something, gave all of myself - worked and worked harder - then finally I would arrive. There would be a destination. It could be cool compactly or ignorance, either way, it's a killer.

I came across an article recently on the New Zealand All Blacks, a formidable, legendary group of modern day sporting warriors. You could imagine that they come from a blood line of fearsome fighters. Their aura intimidates most opposition before the whistle is blown. It was music to my ears, because I feel at times I fight this quest to help educate about the power of vulnerability, when I read about their vulnerabilities.

'A culture of acknowledgement, disclosure and acceptance of vulnerability is actively encouraged. People tend to think that vulnerability and high-performance culture don't mix and that's false. Accepting your vulnerability and having comfort in vulnerability is one method of relieving stress.' Gilbert Enoka, Mental Skills Coach of the All Blacks.

The most used question, which is used daily, is 'How are you?' I find such a falseness in the question, such a lack of meaning and intent. 99 times out of 100, if I was asked that my response would be 'Erm, yeah I'm ok thanks.'

What I've learnt in previous years about vulnerability is just living in the truth. I have a select group of friends, when asked that question, I actually share back honestly.

'How am I? Erm, I'm a little scared today, overwhelmed, got some financial issues. Erm, I've got a lot of pressure about what I'm doing right now, work wise, I miss my daughter, so I feel a little sad around that. I haven't seen my wife a lot this week. I'm tired and I feel a lot of shame that I should feel better.'

Post recovery I've attempted to be this honest. It's really quite fascinating watching people's responses. A shuffling, a real discomfort, a quick change of the subject, and the most annoying - but in fairness, people unconsciously respond to what their subconscious says - is 'You'll be ok. Cheer up, what are you going to do?' Are just some of the responses?

I'm going to do nothing. I'm going to sit with my feelings and try to sit with what's going on that makes me feel this way. What can I control? What can I let go of? Just be really vulnerable and intimate with myself. Into me I see. In-to-me-I-see. Intimacy.

To be vulnerable is to be at risk. Risk of humiliation, risk of physical or emotional attack or both. Today as a coach I sit with my clients and ask them how they're feeling. Sometimes it takes some probing and some more questions, but then we can deal with the truth.

There is no magic potion, silver bullet or magic wand in high performance. All of the people I work with are talented yet they all think the answers lie in getting more talent, working harder, practicing more. I say to them no, you have talent, now we must discuss your dream.

One client said to me they want to be the best in the world. I had to look at whether he has the talent to get there, the God given physical and technical gift. Sure, they can be improved and shaped but to get to the summit, you need some gifts that are big.

In football, I think of Ronaldo, Messi, Best, Gascoigne and all the other wonderfully gifted beings. Now we've got that, we have to create a road map. This map with show us what it will look like daily, physically, emotionally and technically.

Chapter 15-Be More Selfish

If you do not express your own original ideas, if you do not listen to your own being, you will have betrayed yourself.
                                                              —Rollo May

'The truth, the salvation of one's soul is the highest vocation a person can have. Without following that truth, they'll have little or nothing to give. Therefore, our own spiritual growth - our calling - must come first in a necessary kind of self-concern.'   -Unknown Author.

I have a select few books which I use for daily reading - daily realigning with my truth - my armour against the slow pull into my ego that today's world and the unconscious conditioning it creates.

Another quote from an unknown author: 'We are conditioned to believe that selfishness is an ugly word.'

You're so selfish. Stop being so selfish. Selfishness is ugly.

Heartbreakingly, my own daughter at aged five told me the last one. The conditioning has begun for her. There's truth, of course, to the statement, but without clarity. I believe some are born with more selfishness. I have only myself and examples of high-achieving clients and friends as reference points.

I've been accused of it so many times by those close to me in my life - managers of teams I've played for also. It always made me feel like such a bad person. It made me feel lonely. I tried to be different, tried to please others, think of others, put them first, but *why* was it such an effort?

It felt like to be unselfish was to swim against the tide; a real battle. I know today the truth of it. Yes, I am selfish. I really own that part of me. All the therapy I've had, all of the hours of vulnerability and self-discovery led to to own that dark side. That side that can piss other people off, disrupt, be labelled aggressive, angry, too much, too intense. It can drive people away.

As the beautiful quote at the start of this chapter indicates, our calling must come first. It's the 'highest vocation'. It's our only job, our first feeling, it's the wind that blows us, that drives us. It's who we are. Turn my back on that and I'm fucked. I'm just a bag of bones waiting to die. I'm useless, lifeless, no good to anyone.

Who am I? Who are you if you do that? Please don't ever, *ever* compromise yourself - your true self. Stand tall; you'll need courage and strength because it'll piss people off and ruffle people's feathers.

'Calm down, mate.' If I had a pound for every time I've heard that one. 'What's your problem?' - That one as well.

In November 2002, I was in an FA Cup first round. It was a cold, wet day - uncompromising conditions. It was one of the 50 matches out of the 500 I played where I was closely aligned with who I was. I was ready. We won the game 3-2. I scored a late winner. I was aggressive, relentless, and brave at the cost of my own health.

The team we played that day were a strong team. The best in league two at the time. They had the biggest budget as well. They had two experience, tough defenders, one of which was an international. I destroyed them. I clashed heads literally. I received the ball under pressure, I chased things down, I scored goals. I was a constant nuisance and I loved doing it. I got fouled, got up and ran off.

When the final whistle blew we celebrated. We were in the second round. It was a big step for a league two team. We were one round away from getting a big tie.

I went to shake the hand of their captain - a tough guy: 'You've got issues, mate. Fucking issues.' He ran off. He didn't shake my hand.
Little did I, or he know but, 4 years from that very day he would sign me in his first managerial role. Today, 2018, he is head scout at one of the world's biggest football clubs.

I remember going home that night and thinking - maybe I do have issues - it can't be right that I just love physical confrontation and that I get an absolute buzz from having our backs against the wall. I love pain, maybe I do need to calm down. But, there's no time for calming down when you're being led by a higher purpose.

These are weak words from misunderstanding souls. The kind of souls President Roosevelt, in his great speech of April 23rd 1910, talks about. His speech called *Man in the Arena*:

'It's not the critic who counts nor the man who works out how the strong man stumbles, or whether the doer of deeds could have done them better. The credit belongs to the man who is actually in the arena, whose face is marred by dust and sweat and blood. Who strives valiantly, who errs, who comes short again and again because there is no effort without error and shortcoming. But who does actually strive to do the deeds, who knows great enthusiasms. The great devotions, who spends himself on a worthy cause. Who, at the best, knows - in the end - the triumph of high achievement. And, who at the worst, if he fails at least he

fails where daring greatly, so that his place shall never be with those cold and timid souls who neither know victory or defeat.'

Passion is selfish and selfless in the same sentence. If your passion is to get personal gain in the way of material wealth and goods then that's selfish and life has taught me that it leads to such temporary satisfaction. If, however, the passion is to change something and to dedicate yourself to a cause far greater. A good, a reason bigger than you. Of course, the pursuit will require great selfishness but the result will be selfless and that's the great misunderstanding for me.

I know in relationships that many times I've be seen as selfish. I am. My passion, who I am and what I'm meant to be will always, *always* come first. It's bigger than me, bigger than the person I'm with. Without me putting me first, I have nothing to give. I'm an empty shell, I'll be vacant and distracted. The truth of turning my back will eat me alive, ruining everything around me and sabotaging my relationship.

I heard a story recently of Alessandro Del Piero, the Italian international football player and highly successful player - he has won World Cups and Champions League trophies. He was recently a keynote speaker at a big event in London. He was there to talk to a corporation about what it takes to be successful as a team at the highest level.

To cut a long story short, his speech was; 'We were selfish. I would say to you - be more selfish.' There was uproar in the room of people. There was gossiping and talking; what a terrible thing to say. How can he say that? This guy is meant to be highly decorated and he has come here to talk to us as a team about what it takes and he has said 'be more selfish.'

Now, I don't think in the event he expanded much further than that but he was on the right lines and he knows what he's talking about. *Follow who you are.* If a team of people follow who they are and does their job, then you're going to have a hell of a team.

You're going to have a hell of a team in a marriage, too, if two people completely identify with who they are and what they need to do. And, most importantly, put *themselves* first.

It's funny but in my work as a coach today, every super high performer I've met is at their core, what the world would consider selfish. All tell me they are labelled that in their relationships to.

To someone without that gift of ambition then, absolutely, it's selfish.

Didn't mother Theresa put her SELF first when she gave her life to serving others. Her self being that inner calling. Wasn't on the other end of the spectrum Steve Jobs selfish when he gave his life to creating APPLE a brand that's change the world. Wasn't Winston Churchill selfish? Ask his wife at that time. Selfish and selfless are actually hugely linked. I would suggest all of these people were hugely selfless as they were led by a calling deep inside to serve.

To give. But In order to serve they had to put that PURPOSE first. They were led selfishly by a purpose driven life.

As I sit here today I am hugely selfish. I am selfish on the time it takes away from my family to write this book. I am selfish when I invest in another project. However I am driven by a huge need to share and to give back, it occupies my thoughts and heart daily. Not for monetary gain not for notoriety, paid that price! No because it's my life energy my force inside. I want to give and give my energy back until I'm done. Until I die.

Chapter 16 - 'You Haven't Had Enough Pain In Your Life'

When we stray from our destiny, we feel pain. When we betray our gifts, we feel pain. Pain is a wonderful teacher. Ignoring it will lead to grave consequences.

"Pain is our greatest teacher." - The Buddha

'He said I hadn't had enough pain in my life that the best players run with pain, head with pain, pass with pain, tackle with pain, that the best people have had pain.'

It was February 24th, 2015. The young man I was working with had just sat with the charismatic German manager of Liverpool football club, Jurgen Klopp.

I personally was - and still am - a massive fan. His high energy, high enthusiasm, chest pumping, authentic style has rejuvenated one of the nation's great football institutions. The late great Scot, Bill Shankly, was the last. It was the Scots soul that was King.

'Well, he's absolutely right. I love that he's said that.'

I could picture the young player sitting in his hundred thousand pound car with my voice echoing all around him from the speaker system. It wasn't his fault, football is a huge global business now. It's not his fault that investment in young players *must* happen to save competitors from stealing such assets, its simple business or practice.

'Look, I don't blame you mate, in any way. You've been let down by the system. The "pain" that he's talking about isn't physical running, it isn't the fact you haven't been abused physically, sexually or emotionally growing up. I don't believe you have to come from the back streets of Buenos Aires or Nigeria. You're a young man with extra ordinary talent and with huge gifts. I wouldn't have taken you on as a client if I felt deep down you didn't have what it takes to look into your guts and soul and respond. I turned down working with you straight away as I wanted chance to sit with you. To sit away from your agent and family I wanted to dig and probe and know whether it was about the money and watches the clothes and girls or was there a pain. A need, a calling, a place you could use. I could bring you back to. You see I'm worthless to you unless you have that place. Only the best have that place. I had and have that place. I didn't have a fucking clue how to manage such a beast. I looked at mates from council estates and tougher upbringings and thought *that* was the place. It wasn't.'

I continued, 'that place is called destiny and let me tell you a little bit about destiny. Destiny is a place at the end of a road. It's not the final place but, it's a place. Now that place has been programmed into your internal GPS system. Just like before you leave the training ground car park now, you type in an address and your car will head there. Now, here's where we discuss pain! You're in the car and you take a wrong turning and that annoying voice begins. "In 100 yards make a u-turn». Imagine that voice turned up to full volume, it's really loud. Now imagine you don't make that U-turn. Imagine you go straight on. Not for 100 yards but 1000 miles. Imagine that voice, full volume every 3 seconds, saying "in 100 yards make a U-turn" for 20 hours! Oh and imagine you are locked in that car with ho way out! Now, I don't know about you, but that voice would destroy me. It would drive me to insanity. I would want to die'

I was on a roll! I felt this feeling as a player when everything I did was just coming off, I didn't haven't a clue how, today though I know. It's me. No magic formula, just instinct and my gift to communicate, to articulate.

'So back to destiny, destiny is your destination. Your GPS is your instincts, your gifts, they take you there. Sweat, running and fighting are your vehicle. Pain comes every time you turn off course, every time you half get to the line in a sprint, pass the ball at half pace, run at a player without intensity, don't have the courage to take responsibility for your talent and want the easier, softer way. There is never, ever an easier, softer way. That pain that keeps you up at night, that gets pissed off when someone is doing better than you that haunts you like a ghost. Well, that pain can be taken away. You can buy a new watch, a new car, you can get a new girlfriend, go on a twenty thousand pound holiday, buy a new house with a cinema and hot tub and gym, you can drink, gamble, smoke, have sex, eat junk food, have sugar you can do all this stuff and ALL it will ever do is distract you, numb the truth.'

I leant back in my seat, closed my eyes and waited, I know I have just smashed this young soul with a right hook of truth.

'What takes that pain away is two things; 1. Run until you can't breathe, run and run
2. Trust yourself and who you are. Don't try to be like anyone else, be you. If you don't you will fail. The best take risks and work until they drop.'

'You're right. When I'm angry I play really well.'

'Oh I know anger mate better than you can imagine, I used to need anger like a car needs petroleum. I thought anger was *why* I played well.

What a myth. When you use anger you might get a result but then you know what happens? No more anger because now you get praise. Even if anger keeps you going for six weeks it will run out. And then what? Then we are right back here at WHO ARE YOU? What's your pain?'

'I get it mate, I get it. I want it so bad but get confused.'

'That's why you've employed me mate. To lead you to you. I can't GIVE you anything. You have it ALL I can only lead you to you and your truth.

I sit here today with all these conversations I'm paid to have daily with all these creative and gifted humans in the world of football, golf and business and I think of the main thing I try to do.

I lead them to their pain.

'Always keep your step 1 close to you brother.' He said as he put his hand on my shoulder.

I was 3 months out of rehab and an "old timer" as they call them put his hand upon my shoulder as he shared his wisdom.

It was a Sunday night, 9.30pm and we were sitting underneath a church in North London. Tonight's meeting was my favourite. I was in a 'crap' place if I was to be judged by possessions, by stuff. I had no money really, I had no house, I had no car and I was just starting a business but I had myself. I had been enlightened after 30 days in that treatment centre.

The meeting of Sex and Love addicts anonymous had just finished. There was about 40 people In the room tonight. The feeling was electric. Truth, vulnerability, anonymity the cornerstones of this energy. Women, men, corporate power houses, regular guys, cleaners, teachers and ex-footballers. Occupation was of no relevance at all. We were all here for a common goal; to stay sober. Not from drink but from behaviours and from acting out our feelings. Basically, I was beyond insecure so I used women and sex to give me temporary power and the feeling of security.

'You want to grab a coffee?' Mike said.

Mike was 20 years sober in Alcoholics Anonymous and 3 years in SLAA (sex and love addicts anonymous) He was about 60, incredibly intelligent and yet so, so gentle and sensitive. I hit it off with him. I think the gentleness of our spirits connected.

We sat on a couple of chairs, he offered me a chocolate digestive, I accepted.

'You have a power my friend, I can sense it, and you see this programme we commit to, ultimately it's about us understanding our power so we may use it to help others. Selfishness and self-seeking were the route of our troubles. Drinking wasn't my issue, sex or the obsessive need to be loved isn't either. It's all about the loss of self. The false self is my ego dominating the truth. Keep step one close to you because step one is the day you surrendered. The day the ego was beaten. You quit. You gave up the pitiful human will and you said, universe guide me, show me. As you grow in understanding and effectiveness, as you grow in sobriety and the days then weeks and months and years, the ego will grow back. The mind, the brain and its noise. Your step one was a nuclear bomb to that noise. It disintegrated your ego. It's the most tranquil and serene place a human can ever touch or feel. You know that place?

Steve's aura was unreal.

'Yeah I know that place. It's so so beautiful.' I said.

'Stay humble, stay of the earth, grounded, and stay grateful. When great things happen to you, Drewe, and they will happen, when the bank balance goes from minus whatever to plus whatever, when the sofa at your brothers goes to a five-bed house, your £300 per week goes to £30,000 a week, when lonely nights of self-reflection turn to nights next to a beautiful woman and the laugher of children, stay humble. May god bless you, Drewe.'

I finished my coffee. We hugged, I left. I had an 80 mile journey.

8 days later I had a text from a friend.

'Steve has passed away mate. Heart attack. Let you know about the funeral.'

Dear Steve,
Thank you for being a light in the dark, for guiding me. I think about you and how blessed I was to have met you. Such wisdom. Such grace. Such power.
I hope you are still in serenity.

Chapter 17- Self Respect, Lose It, You Lose Everything

Just be what you are and speak from your guts and heart—it's all a man has.

—Hubert Humphrey

Some of us have doubted our inner voice so completely that we abandoned it totally. Many of us have discovered in recovery that by our denial we had violated our inner voice with lies, even to ourselves. Now we question whether we can trust our instincts, and we may not know what we feel. Masculine spiritual recovery is a return to our guts and our heart. Standing up and speaking from our hearts may be difficult at times, but our self-respect rises as we do. That is where we go for our final decision making. We develop better reception for the inner voice as we live in our truth. We accept that we are never absolutely right. We continue with humility, knowing we may be wrong and listening to others and our Higher Power. Yet we must live with our choices.

I will seek the courage to be faithful to my own instincts.

It was 2.30pm, the phone rang. I was in the car again, driving back from a client visit. It's a typical time for me to start receiving calls from my clients. They're all sharing their stories from this morning's training, some good, and some bad, depending on how much they'd turned their back on who they were.

'How was your first day, mate?' I said.

'Good,' said my client, 'I won a lot of the running tests, I trained well...'

'Good.' I replied.

'We have a new boss. He doesn't even know my name.' Said my client. 'When I look at all my work colleagues and the staff, they're hanging around him. They're trying to start conversations and fake laughter. Then, in the dressing room I could hear them saying things like 'I don't know if he likes me' and 'I don't know if I'm going to play this year or whether I've got a future here'.'

'Back in the fish pool, mate, eh?' I said.

'You know what,' my client said, 'I just thought, I've got no interest in you, mate, you don't even know my name. You couldn't be bothered to learn it before taking this job. So fuck you. I didn't talk to him or his staff.' He said.

'I love this, mate! I think you're finally ready. Ready to shine.' I laughed, he laughed too.

Four days later we spoke again. It was near the end of the week now, under the new regime.

'It's laughable.' He said, as I answered the phone.

'Go on...'

'I've kept my head down, I've been focussed, I've trained hard and focussed on myself. I've had a few shouts of 'calm down' and made a couple of big tackles, pissed off a few people, but in an honest way. It was just through my desire to never felt how I felt last year.'

'Great stuff,' I replied, 'sounds brilliant.'

'On Tuesday he knew my name. On Wednesday he stopped training a couple of times and said 'boys, look at this guy, boom, boom, boom, he's there in your face he wants to win'. And today - Friday - he called me in and said he could see that I'll be his captain and he loves the attitude, the running, the energy.'

I laughed again. 'Now tell me,' I said, 'how are you? How are you really? How are you feeling? It's been an emotional week.'

'I feel great. You know what, after the pain of the last 18 months, where I listened to all these people, all these coaches and kept following them blindly. All these chats we had last year about me knowing the answer inside - by the end of the year I finally felt as though I knew the answer. I just think fuck it, he didn't even know my name and now I'm shining he's my mate. Fuck him. It's like all of those soulless girls who hang around the tables in nightclubs looking for a free ride.'

'Amen,' I said. 'Let's get to work.'

Self...belief. Self...esteem. Self...will. Self...ish. Self...respect. This book is all about being the best version of yourself. But, first of all we must understand who we are. Who is your true self? It's the ultimate journey that any of us will go on. Once we know that as well as possible, we must protect that with all we have, with all we are.

You see, it is all we have. You're the only person who is truly going to be present at your birth and at your death. Everything that happens in between those two dates is just all of us using our gifts to put into the stream of life.

My self-had been so lost, so discarded, so abandoned - as discussed earlier in this book - that I had no self-left to respect, so I would disrespect myself daily. How was I ever going to get the respect of anybody else? I would violate my core, my centre. That inner knowledge of right from wrong; I lied, I cheated, I stole, I manipulated, I used, I abused, I physically hurt and intimidated and emotionally raped others. I did all of this because I had lost who I was.

I had to feed the false me. That dark and manipulative dog inside; my ego. My ego needed glory and fame. It needed materialism and power. It needed to feel strong constantly. But, because my true self was weak and broken, my ego was protecting it constantly. Its voice was dominating my thoughts and actions.

I walked into nightclubs and brothels, knowing deep down it wasn't what I wanted to do. That little voice was me. That little voice saying 'Please Drewe, come on man, this isn't you. She'd be devastated if she found out. She doesn't deserve this. You don't really want this. You know this. You know how you're going to feel after. The guilt and the shame. You're going to hate yourself.'

But the ego was fighting for a hit. It was fighting to survive. It would dominate the true me. The true me on a pitch would dominate many of my opponents. There was no self-left to respect. The shame is the killer. The absolute guilt and shame. When you lie, cheat and turn your back on your moral compass it's a scary, scary place.

Ego can carry many people for decades, painting the illusion that all is well; powerful in their titles, in the job roles, powerful in money and possessions. You can feed it with stuff, glory, holidays and Instagram pictures but ego is the worst and neediest addict of all.

Lying in that cottage in the woods aged 33, about to embark on those 30 days, I was ready. I was ready for help, I surrendered. I couldn't live a life anymore based on my false ego, my Dr. Jekyll. I was finally ready to be me, my Mr. Hyde. Over the days, weeks, months and years that followed I started to find out who I really was and where I'd got lost.

I grew in love for myself, I grew in self-esteem. Every night, I sat and wrote where I'd been dishonest or fearful today. Or, what I'd sought to find myself in. I made amends to those I'd been dishonest to. I checked my fears and wrote down what I could and couldn't control. I handed over the rest to a higher power, a higher consciousness.

A day at a time I grew in understanding and effectiveness. I grew as a former athlete by repetitive disciplines and actions. Physically, this would always lead to an improvement in performance and now the spiritual journey was the same, of course it was. We are, after all, three parts; physical, mental, and spiritual. I grew in respect for myself; self-respect was with me for probably the only time I can ever remember. I have it today in abundance. It's a funny irony; the time you most respect yourself, the more others respect you.

Chapter 18- Being TOO Professional Will Kill You.

Over control is spiritually deadening.
As coach I find that making the person understand the only control they have is governed by the beads of sweat they accumulate. The pursuit of perfection is both heavy and restricting. You will always feel less than. Your dressing room, your office, will have plenty of these people

- Drewe Broughton

'Calm down Barney, just relax!' The Great Dane, former Liverpool and Denmark midfielder, Jan Molby, said in a Liverpudlian crossed with Danish accent.

It was 1.40pm and it was match day at Aggborough stadium, home of Kidderminster Harriers Football Club. Today we faced Cardiff City FC in a League Two fixture. Kidderminster were riding high in the football league and in the play offs, there was still a long way to go but, the spirit was good and we were playing some good football. It would be about character, as it always would be.

Jan Molby had signed me just a few months before. I had come on a month later loan spell from Peterborough United. I was 22 and this was a chance, a real chance, to finally find a home and put some numbers on the board; goals as well as senior matches. I needed to get my career going and start to fulfil that beast within that was unaccepting of me achieving anything less that becoming and England International and Premier League centre forward by the time I had retired. I had everything. I was 6ft 3, technically good, had vision, a good touch and I was a really good all round athlete, great in the air, aggressive and super, super competitive. But, I missed the key ingredient: *consistency.*

I would yo-yo between no confidence at all to complacency and thinking I was better than everyone. Such polarity destroyed me. The truth was I didn't have a clue how to manage the beast in me. This drive. So I thought I should do *everything* as perfectly as I could. If my diet, my training, my sleep and my alcohol consumption were all controlled. If I got all the science right and employed people to guide me, then - and only then - would fulfil my talent.

Jan was a great guy and I think if we sat today we would have so much in common. As I would with so many of the coaches who signed me, including Paul Ince, Chris Sutton. These guys, played right at the summit of the world game, the elite level, a level I dreamed of getting to.

All these guys saw that level in me. As a man and leader and also technically and physically as a player. I think that's why it was so hard for them with me, like it was a personal insult that I got complacent and arrogant and then I was terrible and offered nothing.

'Barney' - Gary Barnett was a good man. He had a lower league career, maximized by desire and will and fight. A good foil for Molby.

'Just relax. At Liverpool we weren't thinking about bloody warm ups at 1.45pm! We would be sitting around, reading papers and having a laugh. Five minutes before kick off the newspapers went down and we had a little hamstring stretch and got in the tunnel, won the game and went home. Hey Drewe, its all bollocks.' He laughed out loud.

He was a big man with a big personality; the kind I could relate to. Unlike Jan, though, I didn't know how to be me. He was just himself.

Like other managers in my long career they would use me as reference point because, not that I knew it at the time but, they saw a little of me in themselves.

I smiled and laughed back. 'Yeah Boss.'

Deep down I wish, oh I wish, I could have had that. That ability to just relax like he had done at Liverpool, who, at that time, were the best club side in history. Serial winners.

I sat thinking 'here's me about to press start on my stopwatch and time 30 minutes'

My mental preparation already done:

09.00am - 13.00pm - 2.5 litres of water with 2 scoops of high energy powder.

10.00am - Bath and stretch.

11.15am - Organic peanut butter on rye bread 3 slices, 2 bananas, protein shake.

12.00pm - 12.15pm - Walk.

12.15 -12.45pm - DVDs; Gladiator, Any given Sunday (fast forward to warrior clips).

13.00pm - Drive to stadium.

13.15pm - Arrive at stadium.

13.20pm - In dressing room.

13.30pm - Meeting and tactics.

13.40pm - Change, strap wrists (superstition), oil legs.

13.45pm - 14.15pm - stretch, activation.

14.15pm- 14.45pm - Onto pitch for team warm up.

14.45pm- 14.55pm - Last team talks, match shirt on, sit in toilet cubicle , close eyes and hope, hope I could find it, big loud shouts, getting myself going and 'up for it', high fiving team mates.

14.55pm - Get in the tunnel. I was always the last as didn't want to see the opposition. Stare ahead. Some days shout 'come on boys, let's bully this lot, they're cowards' aurally when I was weak and afraid. Trying to intimidate. A scared little boy, ego in full flow. Or other days just leaning against the wall, nice and relaxed, making eye contact with my opposite number. 'Hey mate good luck out there today' my soul at peace. My mind, serene.

Those were the days. The days I was exceptional. The days I got respect from big, big men. The days I had seasoned international managers just look at me or step out of my way in respect. Just a quiet 'exceptional today Big Man'. On those days I deserved that label that I was called all my career. 'Big Man'. It was more than my 6ft 3 inch, 88kgs stature. I have a huge man inside me; courageous and brave, honest with integrity.

Humility with power. I'm that man today. I'm me. But back then it was a lottery which me would turn up. The real me or the mind-made false version driven by fear.

15.00pm - *Showtime.*

That level of focus would be seen as the ultimate in this science driven world of 'marginal gains' we live in today. Driven by data and GPS, so called proof and evidence. All these scientists fresh from university, full of theory and books. With Zero knowledge, Zero awareness of the power of the human soul. That place of stillness that Molby had talked about. The fact that more is less. There ain't no science or data available behind *feelings.*

Molby played in an era when science wasn't about. Where profound leaders like the late, great Bill Shankly drove the standards. Keeping it simple. Play at speed, small sided games 5-a-side, 7-a-side, run until you can't breathe, get a solid team spirit. A dressing room with character, fight till you die. Go home, sleep, and wake up, press repeat. Do it every day. Retire. Die.

Science has done so much and changed the face of the world as we know it but, it was the great Winston Churchill who said post war in his Middle American speech. 'The world needs scientists but we don't need a world full of scientists'. The genius inside that statement typifies the "greatest Briton of all time".

Back to that day against Cardiff City FC.

I had formed a partnership with a new recruit. A Danish player. Bo Henrikson, my polar opposite. Small in stature, no eight pack, pecs and thigh muscles glistening in oil. No protein shakes or organic peanut butter rye bread sandwiches consumed exactly 4 hours to the minute before kickoff to maximise absorption.

Bo had long blonde hair half way down his back, on matchday it would be out in a ponytail with a stray elastic band that sat on his wrist the rest of the week.

Bo Henrikson, the relaxed Dane of whom I was so envious

Bo lived in a flat with no flash sofas or TV, he didn't own a car, he never had new clothes in fact, and, I say this only as an observation and in *no* way a character reflection, he often looked like a homeless tramp. But, boy could Bo play. I was jealous of all he was. Jealous of his humility, jealous of his carefree spirit, jealous of his relaxed attitude and his ability to have the ball anywhere on the pitch. Most of all I was jealous of his goal scoring record. He banged in goals left right and centre; volleys, tap ins, 20 yards out, free kicks - every type.

I knew if I could just find his relaxed approach I would soar to the top. My physique, my power, my athleticism. The tragedy is, I never did find it for more than a dozen matches in any one year.

Last week I heard Chelsea and England's super talented midfielder Ruben Loftus Cheek talk of the great Spaniard, Barcelona midfielder, Sergio Busquets. He said: 'He's unreal, he has the ball all over the pitch. He's never flustered, never rushed, what a player. But, he's skinny and not that quick and it makes me think if I could add that to my game with all my power and strength and athleticism; wow, I would be unplayable.'

I thought instantly of Bo and myself.

Loftus Cheek after years of searching for himself and for peace, scored a hat trick for Chelsea recently in a European match, I thought to myself; I hope he managed to add the ying to the yang. If he has then the country has a world beater.

I never managed to.

It wasn't just this day at Kidderminster. It was every day and year of my career as I searched and searched for the lost child, the lost instinct. I searched to find that player in me, that man in me that was always the best from 8-18 years of age. Ten years of being at the front.

A year later at Roots Hall, home of Southend United Football Club there I was, 1.45-2.15pm, sat alone in the gym under the main stand. Just me, my focus, my plan, my routine and my fear.

The youth team boys at Southend, the 16-18 year olds all trying to become professionals would huddle in the corner eating Mars bars and having banter avoiding their match day 'duties'.

One of those boys was my "boot boy" at that time. He was assigned to look after my boots, make sure I had what I needed. A good grounding and a chance to watch a professional first hand conduct himself.

Michael Kightly was a winger, rangy but talented. He had already played in the first team. We had become mates despite the age gap of 8 years and our status difference.

Mike went on and had a brilliant career. He was released by Southend United because they thought he wasn't good enough. He bounced back and represented Wolverhampton Wanderers, Watford, Stoke City and Burnley FC in a 17 year career with a decade in the Premier League. Now he's back at Southend United to finish a brilliant career. A year ago Mike honoured me by accepting my Invitation to be my best man at my wedding.

In his speech, which was brilliant, Michael referenced this story and the guests loved it!

'I was 16 and Drewe, who was the main man at that time, was in the gym before the game doing weights. I said 'Drewe, what you doing?' He said, 'I'm getting ready!' Now I was a young lad looking to see how professionals did it but even I remember thinking, that ain't right, weights before games, what's he doing?'

My best man Michael Kightly sharing this story at my recent wedding

Michael Kightly playing for Burnley in the Premier League

What I have learned, is that the gift is the curse.

The gift of desire and ambition can burden you with voices that intensely manifest and drag you to needing more proof. Today I say to guys, once the work is done, not too much work, not too little, you *must* let go.

Sit and don't isolate yourself with all this white noise. Just have one goal, to give your best, run till you cant breathe, in the corporate world, make calls, have meetings, send quotes then let go. Maybe, just maybe, you're good enough.

Chapter 19- There's no finish line

It's my belief without all doubt, that in my final hour I will face a simple truth. Did I follow my path , my heart more times than I didn't? Trust myself more times than I didn't? ' So get up and go again'!

- Drewe Broughton

And Then What...?

'What the fuck are you doing?'

It was a cold November morning, the frost patches that remained, protected by the shade around the perimeter of the training ground showed the temperature. The sky was bright blue and the winter sun, although low in the sky, was shining.

Nineteen footballers formed a circle, black training kit on, in the middle was Fitness Coach, Russ. He was ex-military; a good guy. He loved physical pain and fitness, it was befitting of his role.

'Right groin stretch.' Russ said.

The players switched from a left groin stretch into a right. There was a sway as everybody shifted their body weight. That's something that would've usually caught my eye. But today, unlike me, it didn't. I was mid-conversation with a team mate about Saturday night; the usual banter. We were throwing back and forth some funny anecdotes, none that I even remember now.

There wasn't an issue with talking at all. You could hear pockets of conversations between the lads as we mirrored Russ in the middle. As long as you did your work, that was kind of the mantra. All of a sudden, a familiar voice broke the still morning.

'YOU.' I still hadn't twigged. As I looked over I saw the boss pointing in what seemed like my direction. I say 'seemed like' because I was a great professional; sometimes I could be too serious and too focused. It was my downfall, really, but it meant I was diligent in my work. After 13 years as a player, it was never me a finger was pointed at.

'Drewe, what the fuck are you doing?'

He now had my attention. Being as sensitive a guy as I am I blushed heavily.

'Everybody is doing a right groin stretch apart from you.' I looked around, it was obvious. 'That shit costs you championships. Go ! Fuck off over there with the youth team.'

I didn't hesitate. It was November now and these standards had been implemented since July. When Paul Ince walked into the club there was no grey area. He gave everyone the rope and slowly players hung themselves, dropped the standards, didn't have the self-motivation or will to do the shitty stuff. The discipline, the detail and the sweat gets lost. We're in a society - especially in football - where these principles, amongst others, are seen as old school. Two words that to these new breed of scientific coaches screams inadequate, not trendy; ugly, even. Fucking clueless.

As I stood straight from the stretch position, I saw the canteen window that overlooked the training ground slam shut . I started to walk over to the youth team who were training about 400 yards away. As I started to go, the boys whispered the usual banter. They were a great group of lads, but out of the eyeshot of the managers prying eyes.

'See you mate.'

'Bitched.'

'Enjoy your session.'

I deep down love that from them! I gave them the mornings entertainment and also served a stark reminder of the standards that were in place. No grey area.

As I walked across the training ground, the grass glistening from the melted frost, the air in my lungs was clearly visible as I breathed heavily and upped my pace across the training ground, not wanting to appear sloppy. My head was on fire; 'cunt' ' Who the fuck is he anyway? I'm the best pro here. So what I was slightly late changing position'?

Ah, my ego. That pathetic, man-made little protective shell we use to protect us from the brutality of the truth. It's like ripping off a plaster on a wound not fully healed. The truth can be too painful for many. Yet, if we leave the plaster of the ego on, we're destined for a life not lived. The truth, for so many, is just too brutal - it was for me, for many years.

This sums up why, today, as a society we're in denial. These systems we have in place - that generally dominate - from schools to academies to families that encourage an easier, softer way. You don't get anything with an easier, softer way. I've always had a very powerful moral compass, a real leader in my very being. He was quietened though, through self-doubt. The true me caused my ego so much pain. My persistent nagging and alternative voice was like two fighters sparring constantly. It's the true self vs. the ego. My true self, stripped of any armour, is just a quiet, knowing presence. Like Achilles in the start of Troy; when Brad Pitt takes on the toughest warrior in Greece with just his ability and no armour.

My ego couldn't cope. He was eliminated in seconds. Vulnerability, trust, faith; the things I could never grasp and hang onto. But that truth soon kicked in during that walk across to the youth team training pitch.

'You've got to stop this. You're not even in the team right now and the boys are winning every week. You think you can have 10 seconds off? He was at Man United, Drewe, for over 7 years. He won everything. He was in a dressing room full of leaders and serial winners; Keane, Robson, Hughes, Cantona, Giggs - and with Ferguson at the helm. He played a game in Rome as captain of England, blood all over his face and shirt. He's a winner. You're fucking wrong, mate.' My true self jolted me back to reality just as I heard the voice of the youth team coach.

'Hi Drewe.' Said the youth team coach.

'Hey. I was fucking around and the boss said I have to train with you guys today.'

'Sure, no problem. We're just going through these passing drills. Join in, jump in behind Kieran.'

The session went by pretty quick. The truth resonated and I took the standards it meant to have a professional career over to that session with the young hopefuls. They were miles away from the standards being set only 400 yards away. No more than a Rory McIlroy driver separated kids with dreams with serial winners and yet the gulf was enormous.

I punished myself after the session. I did fifteen box to box runs and seventy yard sprints. It's who I am at the core level; a winner. I'm brutally honest and accountable.

I walked back to the changing rooms with a bag of balls slung over my shoulder, I was helping the youth team coach wind the session down. The boss walked towards me. I felt that fear you feel when the headmaster is calling you to his office but as I looked up, he grinned at me.

He put his arm on my shoulder, 'don't get sloppy, big man. I tell the young ones to watch you. You set a brilliant example every day. You've got a good work ethic. You're first in, last away. What you lack in ability you more than make up for with your attitude. You can't afford to drop it for a second, like a cancer and all of a sudden you start not quite getting there in a sprint, not quite getting the pass in. Overnight you'll lose points, you'll lose titles, and you'll lose cups. Worst of all, you'll lose your position. I paid a huge price for that at Manchester United. I got too big for my boots. Boom, I was gone. Now, get in there and don't let it happen again.'

'Thanks boss.' I said.

I remember driving home that afternoon - it wasn't far, just twenty minutes - but it was a nice drive through the country lanes. I was reflecting. Wow, I thought, I've just learnt gold dust today. In thirteen years I've never been exposed to such standards. See, I think humans - as a default - have a streak of laziness; an easier, softer way is sought. It's not a negative. I think it's just the way it is. The killer for me was the pressure I put on myself. It was never looking for an easier, softer way. But, that day I'd learnt a hell of a lesson; there is *no* easier, softer way. There never will be. We wake up, we press start, we finish our work, we press stop. We relax, we switch off. We spend time with family and friends. Then we sleep, we wake up, we press start, we go again and we press stop. It goes on, and on and on. There's no finish line. We can quieten the noise of our heads tricking us into the 'it's more than that, that can't be enough'. It's the ultimate process and it's what I lead with today. It never gets fucking easier, it just is. It's in your work life, in your home life, in your fitness, in your spiritual fitness, in your relationships; all components that make our lives up. It's brutal, hard, disciplined work. Switch on, switch off. When I hear that voice inside now saying 'come on, mate, you're shattered, cancel the client.' I tell it, 'fuck you, you'll destroy where I want to go. Get back to the line, Drewe, and go again.'

Chapter 20- JUST DO IT

'At aged 4 you just did it . Aged 5 the same . By 10 still , you just did it . Now here you are at 22 overthinking. One foot in Tomorrow and fear constantly'.
'So what do I do'?
' Just do it, just be you and let go of what that might lead to'.

- Drewe Broughton

I started this book with a story. I'm going to finish it with a couple more. The start was from a dark day in 2003. These ones from more recent times in 2013 and 2018.

'How's things mate?' I asked, 'hip ok?'

He was 19 and a really talented young golfer. As one of the country's leading amateurs, he turned professional six months before. I had helped with a hip issue and been offering him strength and conditioning solutions more relative to the golf swing than the generic strength work he had been served up previously.

'Yeah hips really good mate, swing feels really good but...'

'Go on mate, but what?'

'Well I'm taking a few weeks off, to be honest. I've missed the last 6 cuts and my heads a bit fried.'

'Ah.' I sympathised.

I knew that place well. I'm merely a keen recreational golfer. I don't know what it's like to stand over a putt with it all on the line. To stand on a tee with trouble left, trouble right, two shots off the cut and knowing I have to maximise this par 5 and get a birdie. Swing thoughts. Past pain. Fear.

Fuck Everything And Run.

I thought immediately how lucky he was he could take two weeks away from it all. What I would have given for that mid-season, out of form, head full of voices and having to go out there and pretend all was well.

You get a lot of amateurs at various sports serving up solutions to professionals. I say this not from a place of ego. Just truth. For me, the minute you decide to get paid for something. The minute you rely on your talent to create financial security for yourself, your family and beyond, you open the lid on a box. In that box are a thousand voices.

It's no longer just about having a laugh. It's now serious. I think of Jimmy Bullard, the footballer, in more recent times. I don't know Jimmy and he had a brilliant playing career. The thing that jumps out for me when I think of him is the fact that from amateur to playing in the premier league *he didn't change.* He was like this is me, this is what I do. I run around, love playing, have a laugh, a joke and just do it. I must say that is a great quality. Whether that comes from a place of ignorance, lack of real sensitivity or just a great strength to know changing would destroy him, it's the most powerful thing.

'You're my last client today.' I said, 'do you want to go and grab a coffee and have a chat rather than work physically today?'

I knew better than any man. I knew the myths around making yourself physically and technically elite if the captain of my ship was asleep at the wheel. My captain kept falling asleep after spells of sailing like a champion through the stormy waters.

'I think I might be able to help you mate. I know we have traditionally done physical stuff but, I realised when coaching a team last year, I have a lot to give.'

I didn't know at the time but it was a pivotal moment. For me and for him.

'Yeah, you know what, I would like that.'

'Cool.' I replied. 'Let me pack these bits up and we will go.' I folded up my treatment table, zipped up my kit bag, tidied up some client notes and turned off the lights as we left the studio.

Thirty minutes later we were deep in conversation at a pub round the corner. A flat white, a still water, a pad and a pen. Little did I know this was the start of amazing journey that started five years ago

'I want to do an exercise.' I said. 'I want to take you back, right back because your head is full of shit. Tell me, when did you start playing golf?'

'Well, I was about 10. I had been playing football with all my mates, but my dad always played golf so, I started going to the driving range with him. You know just hitting balls. I liked it.'

'Go on.' I said.

'Well, by 12 I was playing a bit more and I was off about 8 by then.'

'You were off 8 in two years? Had you had lessons?'

'No, no lessons. I just watched Dad and found a swing.'

I couldn't help but laugh as I sipped my coffee. He didn't know it but he was validating everything I believed, had seen and had lived through.

'And Then What? So you're now 12 your handicap is 8. Were you still playing football at this point?'

'No, I was playing less. I loved golf so I started to have a few lessons. Not many just started to understand the game a bit more.'

'Makes sense.' I said.

'So within a year I was off 3 then by 14 I was scratch and by 16 I was up there with the best amateurs in the U.K. I was off plus 3.'

'Fuck me. So from 10 with no lessons, in 6 years you're one of best players in the country?'

'Yeah.' He replied humbly, still not seeing the pattern as I created this timeline in front of his eyes.

'Then what? Did you start playing in events?'

'Yeah I played. I won a few and played for the national team. I financed school at the same time.'

'Then you make the decision to turn pro?'

'Yeah, I was 18 and thought this is what I want to do, got a few local guys to sponsor me, to cover travel, tournament fees and stuff.'

'And here we are...' I said, putting the pen on the paper. 'Can I tell you what I see. I have done nothing more than hold a mirror up, man, that's all I've done. I see talent. A gift. I see a guy who fell into his lane at 10. Who just did his thing. Who soared effortlessly to the top. When I say effortlessly I mean WITHOUT MENTAL EFFORT, and you are smashing it, just doing it your way, then you turn professional, and you stop.'

'When I turned professional I thought ok, I need to go to the next level now, I need to step up. I can't be at world level with what I'm doing now.'

BOOM; that moment. That moment when doubt bullies naturalness. Fear beats trust.

'And my start was ok, I made a few cuts, had a few top 20s, but this last 8 weeks has been shit to be honest.'

'Tell me, what were your thoughts when you used to play?'

'Well I just did it. I loved creating shots and I could just see what was needed, turning it left to right, right to left, I just, I just...'

'Go on, go on!' I said excitedly, knowing the fog was lifting and the way out of the maze was nearby.

'I just felt it.'

'You just FELT it.' I took a big breath out. 'Humans and our feelings and instincts. Thought replaces feelings. And now what do you think?'

'Well now I'm thinking keep it ticking, nothing crazy, make the shot.'

'You're playing safe. You're in a pen with the sheep.'

'The sheep?'

'Yeah the sheep. All trotting along, walking the same, looking the same, playing the same. Look what you did, 10-12, 12-14 , 14-16 ,16-18. You just saw the shot had a great feel. You felt it and now you're thinking it.'

'I am. I am. I've bloody lost it, haven't I?'

'In the fog it's lost yes but we've cleared the fog, man, and now there it is. There's a set of golf clubs standing there next to a tee box, through the fog saying, come on buddy, come and pick me up like the old days. Me and you creating havoc.'

His pale withdrawn face had colour back in it. The frown was a smile, the eyes a dull grey to a blue.

'I'm going to play next week.'

'Go and play mate. Let's speak every day on FaceTime. I want to make sure when the voices pipe up I'm there with a baseball bat to smash them in the face. The fucking sabotaging bastards.'

We both laughed. He played the next week, we spoke, as agreed, daily. He made the cut.
He made the top 20. He made the top 10. He won. There he was with his first win, holding the cup.

I was delighted for him. It triggered years of soul searching I had done. That feeling when you win after a storm, is unsurpassed so far in my life.

I had a vision. I saw myself as one of the best coaches in the world. That day I felt I was on step one. There might be a hundred thousand steps, of·that I don't know but, through all my suffering I had been blessed with an ability to clear the fog.

Five years on from that day with that talented young golfer I found myself sat in a restaurant with the owner and sole director of a city finance company. Like my clients my path was unfolding. No finish line just brutal hard work plus absolute honesty. A simple yet relentless equation.

'Mate, why do you rock back in your chair and go really quiet when the lady brings up the KPIs (key performance indicators) and the stats?'

I took a deep breath. Michael sat there and waited eagerly for my response. As I exhaled (something I tend to do a lot these days. Deep breaths. Seven seconds in, chest fully expanded, seven seconds out. Completely releasing all the air from my lungs.) It was more than exhaling air from my lungs. More than a simple, biological, essential act humans do to live. I was letting go of what was coming next. What was coming was the truth. Well, my truth, not the truth. I'm not an authority on that.

I hope you've been led, in the pages that proceeded this one, through this. My truth is built on solid foundations. Foundations built in honesty, integrity, hard work, loyalty, commitment. The stuff of leaders. I realised in that cottage and during that experience in 2012 that I am one.

Michael sat back in his chair. He didn't force a response but I was ready. Fuck me, the only reason I was sitting opposite him was my truth. The only reason I'm busy today is my truth. The reason I have a beautiful family is my truth. The reason I'm writing this bloody book is my truth. It's all I have to give!

Michael owns a big, city company. He's sole director now, twenty years on from where it begun. He's a really great guy; honest, open, humble, gifted, hard-working, creative, kind, but he was fearful. He'd lost himself. The Michael sat opposite me was afraid. He was lost. Most of all he was burdened by the greatest fear a human being can be burdened by. The fear that locks a metal box around our spirits, our souls and our creative urges. It throws the key up to our brains for us to control. Michael's brain like so, so, so many others in this world was running the show. I knew this because mine did for too many years and you'll know by now the price I paid for that.

You see, our brains, I believe, are an organ. Much like our hearts, our lungs, and our livers and so on. The hearts job is to pump blood. The lungs to absorb and release oxygen. The liver's is to process waste and so on. The brain's function, well, it has many and I won't humiliate myself by trying to name them. I'm not a neuroscientist. I'm a guy who had his arse dragged through many, many, many highly pressured situations and got led to some wisdoms that like it or not, continue to change people's lives 360 degrees, as they have mine.

I do believe the brain has a million thoughts; traumas, lessons, images, information. All the things we read on Google, the TV, the days at home, the days at school and so on and so on. But, as I've established, my brain is not who I am.

'I rock back in my chair and go silent because I don't buy it. I don't buy any of it. I don't buy the KP - whatever they are, the stats, the data.

Look, I'm not an idiot, stuff has its place. Please, indicators can be brilliant. The science can be used, man I use it with my clients. I want their running data daily so I can use it as an indicator NOW and again. Once they've run quick enough and far enough .. AND THEN WHAT..? Then the magic, the gifts, the god damn individuality. Mate it was the greatest Briton of all time, Sir Winston Churchill, you talk about leaders, fuck me, and you talk about pressure. Sure, he had his reports and stats and all the other advice from his generals, but *then what?* He went with his fucking gut, man. His soul. It was his gut feeling he led with. Look , that was who he was at his core. I smoked cigars today, you know. I started about five years ago. They don't take away all my stresses but each breath in and out takes the edge off. You know what it takes the edge off of? Having to live in my feelings. It's fucking lonely. I need courage. So I can picture Winston with his big Churchill in his mouth as he lived in his feelings, in his gut, with the pressure of the world on his shoulders. As he addressed a nation and gave hope to millions of people camped around their radios at home, terrified. And these poor souls on the front line, petrified as well. He gave hope. How? Because he believed it. Not in his brain, his gut, his heart and who he is. So I'm not saying don't have data and KP - what are they?'

Michael laughed, 'KPIs, mate. Key performance indicators.'

'Ok, well, what they're key performance indicators of, I don't know. I'm really aware I'm controversial. I'm flying in the face of all the shit that you've heard. But, I didn't ask to be here, in the city, at 8pm. Me and you. You asked me three months ago on the back of a post you saw me put on social media.'

'Yeah, it really resonated with me.'

'Ah, it resonated, did it? Do you know what that means? And please, I'm here to help you not to patronise you. But, it means to evoke. To trigger images, emotions and feelings. So, what did it evoke in you that day, that post?'

'Well, it triggered how I used to be.'

'Go on...'

'When I smashed it. When it was easy, when it wasn't hard and I just did it.'

And Then What...?

'You just did it. By George, we're there. You just fucking did it, man. I just did it, too. I spent years digging up holes and thousands of pounds looking for answers. I was desperate, needy and afraid. A little lost sheep on a hill side. The tragedy is, it was only about 5% of the 600 matches I played where I found 'it'. Man, it was effortless, it was good. I was an absolute leader of men. But before I knew it, the chattering monkeys piped up in my brain, my poor spirit was buried again and that was me for six weeks. You just did it.' I sighed.

Poor Michael looked like he'd seen a ghost. The colour had left his face. He shifted uncomfortably in his seat. My head slowly rolled back, my eyes shut and I blew a big lungful of air to the ceiling. I didn't open my eyes for what seemed like minutes, but it was probably nearer twenty seconds. The silence was broken by Michael's voice.

'I'm scared, aren't I? I don't know who I am.'

As my head slowly rolled forward so my eyes were level with his, I said, 'yes mate, there it is. So, who are you? 'I want to do an exercise, if you'll let me, that I did six years ago with a golfer when I fell into this place of being a coach.'

'I want to go back, right back. You are 16. What were you doing?'

'When I was at school there was this young enterprise thing. There was 12 of us and we had to come up with a product and sell it. It was sort of like The Apprentice but the school version. We were all sitting around and I suggested fishing tackle. I like to fish. We can buy second hand tackle from the shop I use. I know there are good margins on it. There's a good market and we can sell it. They went with it, but rolled their eyes. We managed to get to the National Finals and come second.'

'Wow,' I said, 'at sixteen years of age.'

I knew where this was going. I can see it; talent. I was it. I lived it, I felt it. I succeeded and I failed. Look back to the chapter 'And Then What' in this book. I talk about another guy, 20 years younger, but with the same problems. He had been riddled with doubt.

'And then what?' I asked.

'Well, I wanted to work in this bar near me. It was cool bar. I'd get some money. So I went in there, the manger looked at me. I told her I wanted to work there. She joked, 'how old are you? 10?' I was 16, but I looked about 10, I guess. I told her I was 16 and I wanted a job. She said

178

I couldn't work behind the bar, for obvious reasons, but that I could be a glass cleaner. I accepted. Within three months I was behind the bar. The customers loved me, I was flying.'

'The pattern forms.' I said, knowingly. 'And then what?'

'Well, I travelled a bit and then my mate said there was a job with him at this place in London. I'd be selling. It was fun; a great vibe, good atmosphere, good nights out, good banter. There was a lot of pressure but the money was big, so I jumped on it. The boss said to me, 'fucking hell, you look about six. What good will you be?' Within three months I was running the show. I was billing more than anybody.

'What age were you here?' I asked.

'Er, 20, 21.'

'Go on. There's 19 years left between that day and us sitting here.'

'Well, the next company I left and within months it was the same deal. Boom, within months I was the top seller. I went away with a couple of mates. They were in similar industries and we talked. We realised we could set something up between us and so we did. And, here we are.'

'Here you are.' I said, '19 years on, great times, shit times, arguments, disagreements, things move on, directors come and go.'

'Yeah.' Michael said. 'I see what you're doing.'

'Go on...'

'I got lost. Fuck me. From the sixteen year old dishwasher who, in three months, is the main bar guy to a huge city company. Who was laughed and joked at from day 1 and then was the biggest biller within three months.'

'The pattern repeats. All I see in this whole exercise is you. So, who are you?'

A thought triggered my lips to move before Michael had the chance to answer. 'I am that I am.' I said in a really deep voice.

I was trying to sound profound. You see, I knew that voice. I surrendered to that voice in a cottage in the woods deep in the Hampshire countryside with just the sound of the owl tweeting in the background. 'All will be well.' That voice whispered to me on that night.

'I am what?' He said.

'What I'm saying is that it's you. It's you, it's fucking you. Not the you that is consulting stats guys with your KPIs. Not the you that was buying every management book under the sun for years. Not the you that was just like me, digging holes everywhere like a puppy frantically trying to find his bone. The bone I was looking for was my instinct, my gut feeling. Me, on the deepest level, just like you. Fuck me, can you see the pattern? 16 cleaning glasses, 17 main bar guy, 18 top job in the city, 18 and a half best salesman. 19, next job, best salesman, 20, next job, best salesman. 22, you've set up your company and here we are at 41, 90 staff, city offices, and turning over a fortune. I'm going to ask you a question. Did any stats guys help you on the way up? Did you need proof to eliminate the risk from decisions? Did you consult all and sundry? No mate, you just did it. You lived by your guts and heart. Now that that is who you are.

Chapter 21- How can I help you?

Before we can truly lead we must have investigated the deepest darkest places in our selves. We must know who we are. Only then can we ask another
'How can I help you'. With the confidence we can lead them back to the light.

- Drewe Broughton

As we get towards the end of this book I want to tell a story aligned with my biggest belief today as I coach and leader of talented footballers, golfers and business leaders.

It's my belief that so many people in positions of power or leadership do not ask those under their rule how they FEEL. Those struggling with confidence, belief, or whatever the issue is that's manifesting itself in under performance in their role. Whether that's scoring goals, saving goals, dribbling and creating, shooting consistent scores under par, or selling consistently and delivering the targets. They don't ask them *how they are feeling.*

I was 18 and 7 months. It was a Tuesday afternoon and I was sat alone on the bench press machine in the Gym at the Colney Training Centre, home of Norwich City FC.

Only 6 months before I had made my debut for the first team at Crystal Palace FC as a late substitute. A week later on my full debut I scored away at Wolverhampton Wanderers. I had a three year contact with German kit manufacturers Adidas and had been in the 26 man squad, merely 3 months before this very day, for the England under 20s World Cup squad with that likes of Rio Ferdinand, Michael Owen and Jamie Carragher.

So clearly I was a good player. In fact I will go further than that, I was very talented.My greatest gift my insatiable drive and desire . Two years ago that month , aged 17, Norwich manager Martin O 'Neill Walked Into the dressing rooms next door to where I was sat that very day. It was a baking hot July day on that occasion and the reserves were playing Leicester City. Ironically ,O 'Neill, would walk out of Norwich City Six months later and lead Leicester City back to the Premier League. The remit when he took the Norwich Job. There had been a few injuries and I was elevated into the reserves. I had barely been a full time apprentice three weeks. I ran my heart out . At half time he singled me out in front of everyone. 'Drewe isn't it son'? I nodded, red faced and heavily breathing. 'outstanding son. You keep doing that and you'll be in my first team' 'you lot, have a good fucking look at yourselves. This young man has embarrassed you and I'm telling you now, you just won't play if you think that's acceptable to me'

I felt ten foot tall. We won convincingly as the senior players responded.

When I was 16, during the Christmas holidays, I travelled with the Under 16s squad at Norwich City, where I had been a young player since I was 10, to the training ground for a weeks training and assessment. We were the next 'intake'. We were all in our last school year. We had a very good squad of players. In fact from that group of lads there was to be 9 of us who had careers in the professional game. From Craig Bellamy and Robert Green to Adrian Forbes, myself, Darren Kenton, Chris Llewelyn, Darren Way, Che Wilson and other lads.

On the final day we played a game against the staff. The first team staff and youth coaches. They wanted, I guess, to be on pitch level with us, to see how we talked and moved and to get a real feel for what we were about. I scored a hat trick. The next morning we were sat outside on the benches at the old training ground at Trowse, cleaning boots. It was freezing cold but we, like many up and down the country, were desperate to become footballers so it was irrelevant.

The new training ground at Colney was nearly finished being built and the first team lads were using the new pitches already such was the quality of them.

I was aware of a shout. It was First Team Assistant Manager, John Faulkner, 'Drewe, get your boots and jump in here, you are training with us.' I was stunned to my spot and frozen in disbelief. 'Come on hurry up.'

I ran in and grabbed my boots. As I came back out to jump in John's car the sniping started from my 'mates'; 'Fuck off you can't be training with them.' 'What have you done?' There were few 'good luck mate' comments, too, but not many.

I finished that session and I trained well. Norwich were in the Premier League. In three days time they played Everton on Boxing Day at Carrow Road (home of Norwich City).

Colney training centre - Norwich City FC

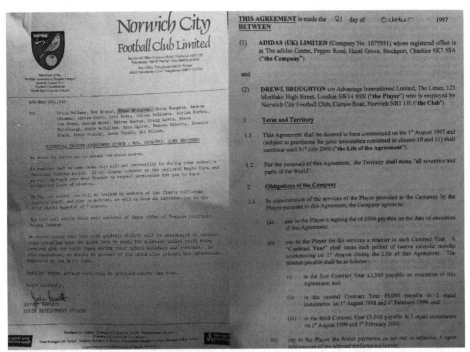

After training was finished ,I was taken back by the staff to get a shower. All my teammates from the under 16s had left via trains and cars back to their homes all over the country. I showered alone my head a mix of excitement and confusion.

Youth Development Officer, Gordon Bennett, came in just as I was pulling on my trainers, it was getting dark and I wandered how I was getting home to Milton Keynes, where I lived with my mum and brothers. I missed the train to Liverpool Street that I caught weekly with the boys.

'Drewe, meet me in the car park in five minutes I'm going to drive you home.'

'Ok Gordon.'

I was really confused now and nervous that I would spend three hours in the car with Gordon. I, like all the boys, had a healthy fear of Gordon. He was a no-nonsense intimidating man but we all had huge respect for him because he cared for us and would do anything for us.

'How have you found the week?' He said in his loud Bristolian accent.

'Um, yeah good Gordon, tough but I enjoyed it.'

'Mmmm.' He said.

Where's this going? I thought, as I kept my eyes fixed on the car ahead.

'You've got a few admirers.'

'Oh ok' I replied.

'Yesssssssssssss' Gordon drew the 's' out. 'They want you to be on the bench on Boxing Day against Everton in The Premier League'

I was rocked. *What?* I'm 16, I'm at school, I'm not good enough, I'm not big enough. A million thoughts flew around my head.

'I told them no. You're not ready. They fought hard, they are really impressed. I told them you've come on hugely this last year and we have high high hopes for you but, this is too soon. Their desperation for points and wins. It could kill you.'

I felt a mix of dejection, relief and confidence. Wow, I thought, me at 16, in the Premier league.

Looking back now how right he was. It's one thing doing it on the training ground it's another thing doing it in the men's game against big powerful men with no regard for my pathetic dreams when their lives were on the line. An attitude I would adopt as the years rolled out. I hadn't been prepared. I wasn't from the streets. I did have a beast in me that could go toe to toe with the biggest street fighters there was. That was much of the confusion that I carried for years.

Wayne Rooney had that naturally. Closer to home so did Craig Bellamy who within 3 years of that very day would score seventeen goals in Norwich City's first team and be signed for six million pounds by Coventry City. 'Bellas' a classic case, a ferocious competitor who was also battered by the game emotionally as he sought to cling onto who he was. He has a huge heart and is a good man who does so much for others.

Back to that day when sat alone In the gym, just me and the laughing pack of dogs in my head. The door opened, I was sat on the Bench Press in between sets of 10, with 70 kgs. The search had begun. Was it strength? Was it technique? Was it speed? Why Can I barely trap a ball?

This search I see today in so, so, so many lost and confused young men.

In walked Keith Webb, my Youth Team Manager. I liked Keith and most importantly, beyond like, I respected him. He was a really good coach. Training was tough and challenging. Sessions were inventive and well-constructed and above all he 'got after us'. He made us graft and sweat sometimes vomit as he attempted to prepare us Minnows for manhood. He knew what was coming.

A player himself he had not made the grade at the same club. He had a good ruthlessness. He was preparing us for what he knew lay over this first summit climb. The mountain range ahead. The lies, the judgement, the injuries, the broken promises, the confidence, the competition and the sheer relentlessness.

He shut the door behind him and stood there looking at me. I hoped he couldn't see into my weak, broken spirit.

His words said he could. They have never left me.

'You know your problem, Drewe?

I didn't have chance to say 'no'.

'You've been used to bullying people on the pitch as you were bigger and now you're getting bullied' He said it in a 'told you so' way.

He turned and walked out.

Keith Webb- Norwich City youth coach in 1996.

It volleyed me in the bollocks.

I analysed the words all night, sat alone in my flat. I'm not a bully, I thought. I'm a good man. I can't have got this far just by "bullying" people? I had a good touch, vision, could score goals was a really good runner, but, yes, I was afraid. Really scared.

But then a voice whispered, the voice we have discussed at length in this book. The voice of truth.

'You have been a bully Drewe, but you are not a bad man, you're a good man, but you are afraid, you have always been afraid and that's what he was saying today that you are afraid.'

Of course that voice was the truth. I was afraid. Afraid of a million things. Afraid I wasn't good enough. Afraid I wouldn't make it. Afraid I was too slow, not technical enough I was afraid of everything. I was so, so afraid.

Fast forward 14 years from that date. Broken, mentally ill, sitting for hours in lay-bys after training just staring. I sometimes cried, but I was long past searching. There was no where else to look. I was at Lincoln City FC.

It was the same scenario. My form was gone. I was so, so broken inside. The Manager was Chris Sutton, a man I had so much respect for as a player. Ironically his father, Mike, had been my under 16 manager at Norwich City. Ironically I was heralded as the "next Chis Sutton" after breaking into the first team at 18. Same position, similar characteristics. I remember the manager at the time, Mike Walker, being asked that exact question. His response has such an ironic message bearing in mind this WHOLE book. He said, 'Drewe is probably better technically than Chris was but, Chris was stronger and more aggressive" his advice to me was to drink Guinness over the off season period. Again I don't blame Mike, not at all, he was merely a product of the system. What I really needed was support and guidance to make peace with and understand that I could be a gentle soul and super sensitive yet still draw on the "killler" I had inside. I needed what I give today. A road map Tony destination drawn out. Day at a time. What I needed to do physically, how to emotionally cope, what it would look like, FEEL like.

Again he had seen me somewhere near my best during a month loan spell from Rotherham United the previous season. It made him really push the boat out to sign me. The tragedy with the disease of depression and mental illness is that it will strip you of all you are and turn you into a shadow of yourself.

Before one game towards the end of his reign, it was a cold October evening at Sincil Bank Lincoln, he turned to me in front of all the players in the dressing room before a the match and said, 'And you, you're getting bullied by defenders every week, you better sort yourself out tonight. You're afraid '

There we are again; bullied.

I was broken. I took it. I had nothing left. I was terrible and subbed off on an hour. At no point did he bring himself to think, 'I'm going to take the big man for a coffee, see how he is. This isn't him, poor guy, I hope he's ok.' I just wanted to be understood, to talk and to open up. The game had taught me long before that day that that's not something you can do.

Suicidal thoughts were entering my head over the weeks leading up to that night. They were reinforced. I craved understanding. I would have played with a broken leg for him.

Me post-match with manager Chris Sutton after another abject performance. I was getting sicker by the day.

Again I don't blame Chris. Another product of the environment. Intellectually, he was and is very, very intelligent. He was a top player with a top career. Emotional intelligence is about empathy and compassion and understanding yourself and your pain to touch another.

I want to put it in writing. I don't blame Keith. Not in anyway. He, like the man I would become, like the majority of the world and certainly the football world, was a product of his environment.

His feelings numbed and buried like mine were starting to be. Another sensitive soul. A good man. He was just a six year old boy, like we all were, locked in an adults body. He had adapted to survive in this culture.

My reason for writing this book was after 25 years in professional football, in every roll, Player, Coach, Physical Therapist and Trainer, now Guide and Mentor I still see the same issues today. All over the world. It's a sickness. A disease.

People at DIS - EASE with themselves. Without the courage or awareness to be true and real through fear of being seen as weak.

I am employed today by individuals, young men like I once was, who sit as I once sat, in gyms, in dressing rooms, on training pitches, terrified in stadiums. Who search, as I once searched. Today however, using technology. Streams of information and "advice" available via YouTube, Twitter and Instagram. So many "solutions". Forums for more confusion. Dangerously in high definition, glossy with incredible sound that draws you in when desperate like moths to a light.

If I was in the game now with what I had achieved from 16 to 18 I would be sat there with a Range Rover and 5 year contract worth a few million. I was an asset. A huge asset. That would have just made it worse because, like my clients today, I then 'look' successful and it creates an even bigger image to maintain.

I am in Keith's roll a lot today. With England youth internationals and young stars. With city executives and leaders. All underperforming, lost, confused and full of self-doubt and hiding behind pillars of sand. Fragile possessions and statuses.

I say to them this:

'How are you man? How you feeling? Please let me help you however I can. I have seen so much pain and so much loss. I have been where you sit and felt how you feel. The fear. The god awful fear that you will never get there. Seeing guys who you know on the deepest level can't compete with you, yet they are where you dreamed of being. That level only you know in your soul you can hit, your benchmark seems so hard to reach again. I will help you with all I am to unlock the padlock you have locking up the true you. That instructive, creative talent behind shut behind ten inch thick steel bars.'

Conclusion

Two days ago I stood on a stage and I listened to the voices inside. The voices I have talked about on every page. The voices that have plagued much of my life. The voices today I know well. Know who and what they are and why they will ALWAYS attack me.

'You can't say that, if you say that you're finished, it's not that kind of place, Drewe. Truth, truth, truth. You and your stupid truth. Who do you think you are?'

'I'm going to come to Drewe Broughton, now. Drewe is a former footballer who today is a high performance coach working with top players and business leaders. Drewe, what do you think are the issues?' The compare for the convention turned from addressing the audience to me.

I lifted the microphone to my lips and as it travelled through the air, my heart spoke; it said 'I haven't dragged you through all this for you to be scared of rocking the boat. Don't mould yourself to fit in. Breathe in and be you. I will guide you.'

'Thank you David for that introduction. So, what do I think are the issues.... ?'
Deep breath....
'So.........'

I finished my talk and was in the room outside the conference suite grabbing a coffee.

'Hi Drewe, I really enjoyed listening to you.' A dark haired lady ,late forties approached me.

'Oh thanks.' I said.

'I must say, though, you still have a lot of anger issues despite all you've been through.' She said. 'I'm Julie, by the way, I'm a sports psychologist and I work at such and such a club.'

'Julie, to answer your statement, yes I do have anger but please don't mistake it as an unresolved flaw. After years of therapy, two sets of twelve step programs, monthly therapy still, childhood issues and career trauma, I am still left with this - as you put it - anger.'

'Then one day only a year ago I realised what it is. It's passion. It's a calling. It's everything I've been prepared for and built towards to this point. There are broken humans everywhere, turning their backs on their dreams and on their instincts, on who they are through others fears and projections.'

'For me to try, just try to impact that in any way, to break through systemic belief systems. I can't be armed with a bow and arrow. I must come with a sledgehammer, a bulldozer of truth of experience, of emotion.'

Julie shuffled nervously. All of a sudden her qualification seems less powerful than perhaps her ego had her believe.

The reason I wrote this book and the reason I concluded it with that short story is because my work day in and out leads me to a universal truth. An epidemic.

Through fear we lose who we are at a core level. It's in the great scriptures. The great wisdoms. The greatest leaders in the history of human kind, all followed and continue to follow their instincts. It's in the marvel comic books that sell millions of copies and whose movies smash box office records.

It's good vs. evil.

It's love vs. fear.

It's truth vs. lies.

It's ego vs. spirit.

It's who we are vs. what the world and it's subtle conditioning made us think we are.

My head is a liar. My heart is the truth.

There's no destination.

There's no finish line.

We can merely wake up and manifest each day with the creativity inside of us all. By following our hearts and guts and by speaking from them, loving with them and performing with them, we have the most powerful navigation system mankind HAS ever and WILL ever know.

Follow that GPS. But be prepared:

IT TAKES THE MOST COURAGE KNOWN TO MAN TO DO WHAT APPEARS TO BE THE SIMPLEST OF TASKS; TO BE WHO YOU ARE.

I would like to make amends to those I am yet to contact.
Those at school I mocked . The coaches and managers I belittled. The players I physically hurt out there on the pitch. Those I made to feel small with my sharp tongue. The girls I lied to. Anyone else that my behaviour hurt in anyway.
I hope you can accept my sincere apology for my part in hurting you. I was sick . I was emotionally un well. All I had was my ego to help me survive and that most vicious and ruthless of predators needs feeding. His food? Drawing and stealing false power from others.
I am truly sorry.

Ron.
(I wrote this poem the night you passed away, the words flowed)
I was only a boy when you came along,

Smiling and happy we all loved Ron.
Full of life and always sharing,
Your time, your money, always caring,
Sharing, sharing, sharing, sharing.

We met at football, you were a dad,
The clubs better players were both your lads,
Bletchley 5 a sides my abiding memories,
Of course you were there on those Sundays.

We grew up, I moved away, turned 18,
Came back one summer, the bright lights I had seen.
You remembered me, said how well I'd grown up,
On the outside maybe, inside still a pup
The next time we met I was turning 21,
A party I had, my brother brought everyone.
We spoke that night, I was lost, full of fear,
I hid it well, sharp clothes, nice car, another beer.
You said "here's my number you need you can call",
A week or so later I had another fall.

So that's where it started your spiritual guiding,
You quickly became the one to confide in.
My fears, my pressures, the voices in my head,
First thing we spoke, and again before bed.
Intense at times, people didn't understand,
Your constant commitment you travelled the land.
Every ground you saw your presence consistent
I fed off your faith in me, as the self-doubt was persistent.

And Then What...?

You had such a gift, the rarest of all,
A deep understanding beyond just football.
You lit up a room your presence so huge,
Made people believe amid life's deluge.
Our bond was so strong the best of friends,
My only wish you lived longer to make my amends.
I owe you so much, not in pounds or in pence,
But, my ear and my time, help to climb one more fence,
For without you there's no way those fences I'd have scaled,
The night at Roots Hall, Don Valley, and I remember Port vale.
With you by my side we were going all the way,
Up from the bottom moving forward each day.
There was one killer, it came as my Ego,
Built on no faith, it destroyed the great show.

I held your hand, the end was near,
Somehow as I sat there I kept back the tears.
"a leader of men" are the words you left me,
I think of them daily awaiting my destiny.
I don't control that anymore, I've found some trust,
In a power out there greater than us.
I don't have much but, then I have all,
The first half my destiny lied with a ball.
Who knows what next big Ron but, I know you are with me,
In morals, in conscience and your greatest gift humility.

We are no more than 5 pints of blood,
Here to help others block their flood
Your legacy, your spirit the greatest of souls,
Put others first help them reach their goals.
I've lost my guide my shining light,
You'll be happy to know I'm scaling new heights.
The ones you knew always were there,
Through loss and pain accepting the flare.
Not with ego or shortcuts nor lies or deceit,
With no more than walking with these two feet.